T0195017

INTO YOUR CHILD'S HEART

Agnes Lui

BALBOA.PRESS

A DIVISION OF HAY HOUSE

Balboa Press books may be ordered through booksellers or by contacting:

Balboa Press
A Division of Hay House
1663 Liberty Drive
Bloomington, IN 47403
www.balboapress.com
1 (877) 407-4847

Because of the dynamic nature of the Internet, any web addresses or links contained in this book may have changed since publication and may no longer be valid. The views expressed in this work are solely those of the author and do not necessarily reflect the views of the publisher, and the publisher hereby disclaims any responsibility for them.

The author of this book does not dispense medical advice or prescribe the use of any technique as a form of treatment for physical, emotional, or medical problems without the advice of a physician, either directly or indirectly. The intent of the author is only to offer information of a general nature to help you in your quest for emotional and spiritual well-being. In the event you use any of the information in this book for yourself, which is your constitutional right, the author and the publisher assume no responsibility for your actions.

Any people depicted in stock imagery provided by Getty Images are models, and such images are being used for illustrative purposes only.
Certain stock imagery © Getty Images.

Cover Design by Karen Lawson-Chipman
Cover Art by Eujin Kim Neilan

All Scripture quotations are taken from the Revised Standard Version of the Bible, copyright © 1946, 1952, and 1971 the Division of Christian Education of the National Council of the Churches of Christ in the United States of America. Used by permission. All rights reserved.

Print information available on the last page.

ISBN: 978-1-9822-3871-1 (sc)
ISBN: 978-1-9822-3873-5 (hc)
ISBN: 978-1-9822-3872-8 (e)

Library of Congress Control Number: 2019919342

Balboa Press rev. date: 11/20/2019

"I learned to treat contraries by contraries."

St. Elizabeth of Hungary (1207–1231)

"There are more things in heaven and earth, Horatio,

than are dreamt of in your philosophy."

William Shakespeare, *Hamlet*

To

Ken and Graham

With Love

To the children:

May their love shine.

Contents

Prologue

Searching for the Center that Creates Harmony

War impacts people. Our human mind sees war as fighting military battles between opposing sides—nation against nation, or group against group for whatever reasons. Disturbing images of rampant violence frighten the viewers. We can control the horror by turning off our electronic devices or not reading the newspapers. We can look away, but we cannot say that the wars don't affect us. They do—it's just a matter of how much.

Unfortunately, many more wars are invisible, fought everyday within a community, within families, within relationships and often within our own psyches. Those battles affect our day-to-day lives, shown in depression, addiction to alcohol and drugs, flare-ups of negative emotions in relationships, mental and physical violence, hate and revenge. This list goes on and on, escalating into increasing suffering of all kinds. Peace is nowhere to be found; love is weak; joy flickers out like a burned out candle. We struggle. We try our best to fix our problems. These wars push us on the inescapable paths of obstacles and darkness. We are lost.

Our children watch these invisible wars fought on borderless fronts. They can feel their effect. Born with the essence of joy and love, these little angels trust their parents to interpret the world to them and make it safe. At the same time, they read the map of their new world on the faces of their parents. Whether it's an invisible war or invisible peace, the contours of their parents' faces express the landscape on an unknown environment. In one of my meditations, I remembered as an infant reading my mother's face, which was filled with sadness and despair. As a young child, I heard my father saying one thing and then doing something else. Neither of them knew that I was closely observing them. What were their behaviors saying to me? Are we parents aware of what we are saying to our children?

Our love gets weakened while we are fighting our own invisible wars. Ambiguous words and confusing actions communicate conflicting directions. What can we say to our children that will make them feel safe and loved? Is there a special place within each of us that has been forgotten, where peace and love can be found? I am searching for this center that creates harmony.

Introduction

Parenting is an intense labor of love, in which we do the labor and we have the love. But what are we doing right or doing wrong? And what is love?

Parenting is a challenging job that comes with no guidelines and no equal exchange. It does not guarantee that your child will fulfill your dreams for him. It requires almost twenty years of childrearing commitment, a high financial cost in today's world, and countless hours of sheer hard work. The moment your child arrives, your life is changed forever. Your priorities are reshuffled. The only guidelines that you have are ones that your parents and predecessors have handed down to you. Family traditions and religion can provide some structure and guidance, but lots of uncertainties remain for parents to struggle with and try to figure out.

Some parents have a good start. They have the resources to raise their children to achieve the American dream of wealth and success. Soon enough, the little protégé will be heading for a prestigious university, and she will eventually become a high-powered executive. Mission accomplished.

But the majority of us walk on thin ice with the hope that our good intentions and efforts will carry us through the journey of childrearing without disaster. We may find ourselves in situations that are far from ideal. There are many weak spots on the ice. An unexpected catastrophe, like a family member's illness or death or a sudden financial loss, could drop the family into the water. And parents with babies who are born with special needs or congenital illnesses face tremendous difficulties every day.

As a clinical social worker that has worked with troubled families, I witness many emotional and mental problems that run across socioeconomic classes and ethnic/racial lines. Families express their inner pain through a variety of destructive behaviors. Advances in medicine have helped to control depression, bipolar depression, anxiety and other mental health problems. Traditional psychotherapy and social interventions are effective in alleviating immediate symptoms. But no one intervention can guarantee long-term healing. Often they are like Band-Aids on wounds that partially heal, but that can potentially erupt again. True healing, full healing, has to come from within the individual.

I left the social work profession years ago, when I decided to be a full-time mother. Before I became a parent, I used to think that I could confidently raise a child. But when I actually became a parent, I was not so sure. To my surprise, parenting was the hardest job of all for me. I was no longer a professional; I was on the other end of the assembly line: a laborer.

Our son came with no training manual or guidelines telling us what his purposes in life were and what specific things we could do for him. We sensed that he was a "unique soul," but where he came from and where he would go we did not know. All we knew was that we loved him.

I really wanted to connect with my son at the heart. Most of the time I did. However, sometimes I saw that I was not fully connected to my own heart. I felt a hint of anger there. There were moments when I lost my cool and said things that I didn't mean. I remember an incident when my son was six years old. I asked him to pick up his toys that were scattered all over the floor in the den. He ignored my request. Then I yelled, really loudly, my voice full of anger. He quickly picked up his toys. Then he asked, "Mommy, do you still love me when you're mad at me?" I was stunned. Of course, there was no question that I loved him very much. What had I said and how had I said it? Where did that anger come from, because it clearly was not caused by such a minor situation?

This incident triggered a desire in me to find that anger. I felt a deep pain whose source was unknown. I was carrying an emotional load of sadness and inner confusion. Parenting is so much harder when the parent is carrying her own psychological load from the past into her present role.

Moreover, I was not satisfied with the conventional rules of parenting, all the rigid rights and wrongs. I had heard old-time mothers who proclaimed with assurance that their way was the right way to raise a child! Coming from a multicultural background, having had an education in child development and mental health, and having my own insights, I believe that there are many approaches to parenting, not just one right one. When I became a parent, I opened many old and new doors and listened to many voices about parenting.

I want to find my own way to being a parent and to be my own person. My anger is sometimes an impediment. I want to find out who we truly are and how to teach our children another way of seeing themselves. I believe that our souls are very much alive and show us who we truly are, but I didn't understand this belief at the time; the voice of my soul had been silent for so long.

As if my soul were calling me in my heart, I began to have a longing for God, who might hold answers for me. I was not particularly religious. I grew up Catholic, attending an elementary parochial school. I also briefly attended an Evangelical church in my teens. My religious experiences gave me few answers that satisfied my longing for God. Eventually I belonged to no religious groups. I wanted wisdom from within.

I embarked on a quest to search for answers. I had no map, no itinerary and no agenda. All I took with me was my curiosity, a seed of faith and an open heart. I wanted answers from a Higher Authority, not from human authorities. To my surprise, insights and answers from Heaven began rolling into my life beyond any imaginable expectations.

1. LOVE IN A CONDITIONAL WORLD

~

On the New Year's Eve, when I was five years old, my father came up with the bright idea of going to New York's Times Square. It was his way of expressing his love and welcoming us, his family, who had just arrived in America from Hong Kong two months before, while he had been in the city for two years. That evening, my older sister and I, along with our parents, braved the cold night, catching the train and walking to Times Square. Time Square on New Year's Eve was the neon-blinking heartland where the bright ball on top of the tall building would come down at midnight. As a petite five year old, I did not feel the joy of standing in the middle of a frighteningly large, enthusiastic crowd with the blustery wind blowing under my coat. The noise, the neon lights, the cold and, even more so, the tall crowd that looked like skyscrapers scared me. I cried. My father's encouragement and my mother's touch did not comfort my distress. I never saw the ball go down.

I have never returned to this noisy and crowded place in Time's Square on New Year's Eve, but I still feel the conditioning of distress and discomfort from this experience. Whenever I watch the Times Square ball coming down on television on New Year's Eve, I make sure I have a warm blanket over me, because I still remember the big crowd and feel the freezing weather.

Conditioning forms the basis of much of learned human behaviors. A Russian scientist, Ivan Pavlov (1849-1936), was famous for developing the psychological phenomenon called "conditioned response." He trained his dog to salivate at the sight of a treat and the sound of a bell. After a while, he just rang the bell without a treat, and the dog automatically salivated. Our sensory system works in similar ways.

In today's world, tens and hundreds of stimuli are occurring at any given moment, affecting the brain and the sensory system to act and respond. I imagine a map of crisscrossed highways going rapidly in many directions, the bombardment of sensory overload: visual, auditory and tactile contacts. From the moment each of us enters this world at birth, these stimuli all work together to mold the individual to think and see life in particular ways. We prefer actions that bring us good feelings and avoid those that give us distress or pain. Like Pavlov's dogs, our nervous system and brain are wired to act and react in ways that we have been trained. This process is called "social conditioning."

Likewise, when it comes to love, situations in the world have made love very conditional. In conditional love a person has to meet many requirements. We are conditioned to love in ways that we have been taught. Early in life, our parents teach us that love has rules. There are dos and don'ts to follow in order to receive love. Predecessors have established those rules with the good intention of preparing us to adapt to this harsh world. If we follow the rules, we get rewarded; if not, we get punished. The reward of love comes in the form of approval: praise, gifts, money, hugs. Punishment includes reprimands, looks of disapproval, and physical/verbal abuse. The reward of love is joy and happiness, while punishment brings pain and sometimes feelings of rejection.

Oftentimes the rules are clearly spelled out, but sometimes they are not. If we do this or that, our parents will approve of us. However, sometimes rules are unclear. We assume that if we behave well, we will get consistently positive response. Then we learn that our parents may not always respond consistently, or they forget to respond. For example, a parent promises to give a reward for completed chores. When a child completes the chores, the parent forgets or changes her mind about rewarding him.

In addition to rules, there are often categories that one must fit into. Those categories grow out of the preferences and cultural beliefs that parents have. For example, a parent can prefer sons to daughters, a specific physical or personality trait, or even a position of birth order. A parent may value a son more, or vice versa; another parent may prefer a child who looks like him, or just the opposite. If a child fits the desirable categories, she receives more love.

The many rules and categories to observe and obey become requirements for love. Those requirements set the conditions for how love is given and taken. Over time, those early experiences of what love is carve deep impressions into the mind and heart of a young child. The five sensory systems—touch, sight, smell, hearing and taste as well as our brain—all together tell us what the reality of love is. We love as if automatic responses are already built in. If we need hugs and approval, we can act nice. If we are in a bad mood, we misbehave and likely receive punishment.

Confusing Rules

Conditional love is what we primarily know on earth. To get love, we must work to earn it. The family is the first classroom that teaches us what love is. Love is based on our experiences: the ways our parents have treated us, how they have treated one another, and how siblings treat one another. Those experiences set the mold for how we give and take love for the rest of our lives. We seldom question our practices and beliefs.

Early in life I learned that I had to earn love through work and obedience, as traditional Chinese culture teaches. Children are to respect and obey their parents and elders without questioning. The practice of unquestioned obedience is indoctrinated into children starting in early childhood. My mother, who was a schoolteacher, read us Chinese children's stories that teach respect for old folks. Children are expected to help elders, obey rules set by parents, and even let the older siblings get the better treats. (Giving the better share to an older sibling is a hard concept for American children to understand.) In turn, children receive love as approval.

While earning love through obedience, there are some categories that I could never fit into, regardless of what I did. For example, within the traditional Chinese family structure, respect is given in accordance with the hierarchy of position: first to grandparents, parents, the oldest sibling and sons. In my family of origin, I was the middle child, a daughter with an older sister and a younger brother. I didn't meet any rank of respect because I was neither the oldest nor the favored son. The only role left for me was as the family's designated caregiver, and I was given recognition only for taking care of others. To me as a child, love seemed vague and unreachable.

In grade school, I learned that love, in form of approval from the teachers, was also elusive. There were too many rules to obey and follow. Teachers gave positive reinforcement to the smartest students in the class. In the world of competition, there would be a few who were ahead, many in the middle were left ignored, and the few unlucky ones at the bottom of the class were shunned.

While conditional love can be elusive, it also can be deceptive and selfish. I watched a Korean movie called "The Treeless Mountain" about two little girls, ages eight and five. Their single-parent mother abandoned them by sending them to live with an aunt for a while. The mother promised to return when their big red piggy bank was full. The girls were expected to make money by doing chores for their aunt. Their aunt gave them little money for the chores they did. Then the girls found another way to fill up the piggy bank. That was to sell roasted crickets as snacks for schoolboys going home from school. When their piggy bank filled up, the girls waited every day by the bus station for their mother to return. While waiting, they built a mound from dirt to symbolize their hope for mother's return. But their mother never returned. Later, she sent a letter asking the aunt to take the girls to their poverty-stricken grandparents in the remote countryside. Eventually, the girls gave up hope. They offered their money to buy their grandmother a pair of much-needed shoes. These unlucky girls met the requirement of filling up their piggy bank, but their mother still did not love them. This kind of love is most unfortunate.

As for myself, I remember that my parents occasionally praised me for being an obedient caregiver, especially when my mother needed help. The praise was modest and quickly forgotten in a busy household of three children. In my then ten-year-old mind, I thought that the standards of good behavior seemed unclear and inconsistent. The standard was in accordance with the shifting moods of others. Parents and adults said one thing but meant something else.

For example, parents might threaten punishment to stop a behavior, but seldom would follow through. In another situation, they set a rule for one child that does not apply to another in the same family. While my mother was at work, she required my older sister and me to make sure our much younger brother drank orange juice. Yet, when I asked if I could have a cup of milk or juice with dinner, my mother sometimes yelled at me.

Re-examining Conditions

In my heart, I did not understand why love was conditional, given to a select few. I was skeptical of this belief that only a few chosen individuals were worthy of love. In the summer, just before I was to start college, I tested this belief. I volunteered in a daycare because of my love for children. Within weeks, I realized that I loved every child in that room. Each was unique and deserving of love and respect.

From then on, I began to take a closer look at what love is. In the distant corridor of my memory, I sensed vague feelings of a place where everyone loves each other unconditionally. This unconditional love seemed free flowing, as if the wind was gently blowing into me. I wondered why it is so difficult for people to love one another on earth.

In my mind as a young woman, I was determined that when I got married and had children, I would make sure everyone in my own family would love one another. When our son came into our lives, we loved him dearly and we felt his dear love for us. When he was a baby, I sometimes intuitively sent out the same question into the "Air": "What can we parents do for him?" The same telepathic answer came back each time, **"Give him lots of love."** I did not know then who spoke to me, but I clearly heard it.

This advice is great, but what does it mean? To conceptually love your child is easy, but to translate idealism into words and actions is not. We place requirements on the translation, filling words like "must, should or ought to" with ambiguous rules that we have learned from our experiences or made up. The requirements act like bricks that we use to build walls between one another. Our words imply, "We can't love you because you did this or that, or you don't do such and such." We also place a value system of good, bad, better, or less or more on the requirements. "We can't love you today because you have been bad. Maybe tomorrow when you behave better." We might make a promise to love that person tomorrow, but when the next day comes, we may have another excuse to push that person away. We can't love that person who cannot meet our requirements or conditions.

What if love had no conditions? What would it feel like? I remember an incident with my then five-year-old son. Just before Christmas, we moved from Boston to the Bay Area outside of San Francisco. For most parents, Christmas is the time to instill good behaviors by telling children that Santa won't come if they misbehave and that Santa is keeping a list of good and bad behaviors of every child. That particular time, I noticed that my son was closely inspecting the fireplace in the new house, which looked very different from the one in the previous house. He curiously looked up, down and sideways examining the structure. One day, I asked him what he was doing. He contemplatively answered, "How can Santa come down chimneys of so many different sizes? I don't know, Mom. Is Santa real?"

I replied, "What do you think?"

"I don't know. Tell me the truth, Mom! Please...tell me the truth! I think there is no Santa, and parents give kids the presents!"

"Well, I don't know about this," I said, hoping he would change his mind.

Several days later, a UPS truck passed our house. I asked him, "Do you think that Santa sends his presents by UPS?"

Having already made up his mind, he said, "No, Mom, parents buy the presents. Now I know that I don't have to be very good." Our young son understood that we loved him unconditionally, and therefore, the love was not based on good behavior.

To me unconditional love feels as if I am running freely in a beautiful open meadow, while conditional love feels as if I am in a small dark room full of fragile vases. One wrong move and I could break them and get into trouble. Whatever labels we put on love, for certain, we all desire the kind of love that helps us to grow and learn from our mistakes. We also wish to feel its safety. No matter what mistake we make, it is forgivable, and the true nature of love can heal the pain and fractures in human relationships.

On the other hand, conditional love is contradictory. John Lennon beautifully expresses the sensuality of love, "Love is touch; touch is love." Love can be so simple and tangible. Yet in another song, he sings,

"How can I give love if love is something I ain't never had?" Conditional love holds many contradictions that make us confused and insecure, along with attaching to us the insatiable desire to have more love.

Experiencing conditional love in this conditioned world reminds me of my first experience at Times Square on New Year's Eve. The excitement of glaring lights, a cheering crowd and cold weather were much too uncomfortable for a sensitive five year old. To me, the joy of New Year was lost in this clamor. The many conditions of love in my life also blared at me like blinking lights with mixed and confusing messages. Growing up, I did not feel the joy of love getting into my heart.

2. EVERY CHILD NEEDS LOVE ON EARTH

~

As a child, I could not feel the joy of love in my heart because there was too much confusing noise in my environment, the noise of criticism. I don't remember the exact wording, but these criticisms had the same message over and over again: I was not good enough. However, as young as I was (less than ten years old), I also knew that every child who comes to earth needs love. From time to time, I vaguely remembered a beautiful faraway place of unconditional love. Sometimes, I imagined being an angel flying, looking down at earth. Once in a while, when I looked up into the night sky, peering past skyscrapers and the dusty lights of New York City, I felt closeness to the stars and the moon. Where did such imaginings come from?

About age six or seven, I thought that I did not belong on earth and was puzzled as to why I was here. I started asking my mother over and over again, "What is the meaning of life?" Annoyed with my repeated questioning, she told me to stop. She said, "There is no meaning in life. Now eat your dinner!"

The meaning in my mother's life was likely just as puzzling as mine, if not more. She grew up in the frightening environment of the Japanese invasion of China, as well as in poverty, when every bit of provisions was rationed during the war. My mother spoke of the frightening sounds of sirens to warn them of Japanese bombing attacks. Teachers and students fled to the nearest cave for protection. My mother also told painful stories of how, in the midst of limited provisions, her mother gave the best food to her grandsons rather than to her daughters, my mother and her younger sister. The blaring sounds of bombs, hunger and deprivation were everywhere. Did my mother feel the joy of love against this background? I doubt it.

My father did not fare much better. He did not struggle with hunger, but he and his classmates along with their teachers in high school took trains from one city to another to escape the Japanese invasion. Wherever they stayed, they set temporary shelter in order to continue their education.

I think of children today in war-torn countries and of those who live in dire poverty. If these children are lucky to have parents, they struggle day to day just to survive, never mind about expressing the joy of love. These families have little joy in life. The harsh reality of providing basic food, shelter and clothing is hard enough, let alone nourishing their children with love.

Even without war or poverty, every child needs love, which is as important as food, clothing and shelter. Since love is an invisible commodity, the nourishment of love can slip by or never reach the child. When a depleted environment has limited resources, love has to be rationed too. Like rations in a war, the many conditions of love are given in measured amounts.

Mother Teresa (1910–1997) said, "The hunger for love is much more difficult to remove than the hunger for bread." The psychological hunger for love can last a lifetime if it is not satisfied. This psychological hunger for love does not always revolve around the lack of basic material needs. It can come in the form of not fitting into particular requirements for love. I am not talking about misbehaving and being punished as much as being put into categories of social values, such as approval or disapproval.

In the traditional Chinese culture where boys are favored, girls are shortchanged and often regarded as second-class children. Boys receive special and extra privileges for they carry the family wealth and honor. Love is rationed, and second-class daughters suffer a psychological hunger for love. Growing up, I did not need high intelligence to figure out that Chinese mothers lavished more loving communication on their boys, who got more praise and treats. My own mother was no different when her son, my younger brother, was born. I loved my brother and sister equally, but I did not understand why society treated genders differently.

Beginning at age ten, I fantasized about building an orphanage for unwanted Chinese girls. In my lonely free time, I designed a building plan to house those imagined unfortunate girls. As the director, I would give them lots of love and provide them with educational programs. By age twelve, these fantasies convinced me to go into social work, where I thought I could put my compassion for unwanted children to work.

Children's Prevalent Suffering

I have always felt tender compassion for children and teens. Every child needs the opportunity to know that he is lovable, but I saw the prevalent lack of love on earth. When I entered college, the studies of psychology and human development, especially child development, fascinated me. As a college freshman, at the college daycare doing a class assignment, I observed an unhappy two-year-old girl with no smile on her face. She went about her activities with emotional detachment. I learned that her parents were highly educated professionals with demanding careers, but heard no other details to explain her unhappiness, which was not part of my assignment anyway.

Throughout my years of experience working with children, teens and families as undergraduate and graduate student and as professional social worker, I saw a broad profile of clients from many different backgrounds. They were of different races, social classes and cultures and had a variety of mental health problems. I have seen families on skid row, living day-to-day, barely surviving, let alone placing much interest in their children. I have seen families showing off their wealth and social status, only to hide their neglect and psychological abuse of their children. Most parents are caught in the middle, just doing their best for their children with whatever resources they have.

Here are some profiles of children with whom I worked who were under stress. In a day-care setting, I worked with a two year old who threw temper tantrum each time his mother left him in the classroom. This behavior was related to separation anxiety over his parents' divorce.

I also observed a three-year-old girl who had difficulty adjusting to preschool and playing with other children. In her play session with me, she moved all the toys to one side of the room, then to the other side and back again. In the process, she exhausted herself and broke down in tears. The moving back and forth reflected what was going on in her household because her parents were separating and moving into different households.

A seven-year-old boy stopped talking after a traumatic house fire. His condition was called "elective mutism," which in clinical terms means that the child chooses not to speak. Another boy, a five year old, frequently and aggressively picked on other children, but he couldn't get enough bandages on himself. One day, he insisted on putting a bandage on his bottom. His teacher discovered bruise marks on him; his father beat him at home.

In another case, a mother suddenly abandoned two young children, ages five and seven. Their father then left them in the care of an elderly grandmother. The older girl drew pictures of an idealized happy family. She told me that her mother would be returning soon.

I also remember a teenage boy who, while he was under protective care, was raped by his foster father over a weekend. This vulnerable teenager's single mother had been neglectful of her children and suffered from depression.

These brief sketches show only small strokes of the bigger picture of the plight of children and teens. Treatment and intervention are necessary for such people, but that treatment does not assure positive long-term changes. At best—my love for children, my professional skills and hard work—all appear to be Band-Aids on chronic problems. Every bit of intervention helps, but over the length of childhood, a few months or even years of assistance can only partially help a child and her family in the healing process. What happens after the intervention and treatment, most professionals can't be sure. In the case of the maternal abandonment of those two young children, I brought needed services to them. However, I could not bring back their mother, keep their grandmother from dying, nor keep the father from neglecting them.

My intention was to alleviate children's suffering, and I saw too much suffering. The social service system is imperfect, as it is usually overloaded and has limited resources. The juvenile justice system is imperfect, even though it tries to work for children's best interests; probation officers are weighed down with many difficult cases. And, sometimes, medical treatment cannot save a child's physical life, because when the child goes home, the care might be left to mentally ill parents. No one professional discipline alone, not social work, not the juvenile system nor the medical system, can solve children's problems. But all of these disciplines are important and necessary to alleviate some of their suffering.

Any early intervention and continued support can make a difference for a child and her family. For example, with some positive social and academic experiences, a shy child can gain confidence and carry this confidence into other areas of her life. However, progress does not go in a straight line, but rather zigzag. Oftentimes, it can take a community to ensure consistent progress. I remember a case in which three teenage brothers were doing well because the school and neighbors genuinely cared about them. Their mother had a long history of psychosis, and their father provided for his family but was emotionally distant. The whole community helped the boys.

On a personal level, I felt as if I thrashed through the rain and mud of providing services only to see a bottomless sinkhole of human suffering and the paucity of love everywhere. I saw the heartbreaking plight of innocent children. Children are the most vulnerable members of society. Their suffering reflects the long-standing suffering of the parents, whose own difficult personal history also speaks of their parents' suffering. Everyone's suffering seems to be connected with another's and another's, over many generations.

I experienced just a segment of society where suffering among children was prevalent. I wondered if it was possible to have healthy families, and my own happy and loving family. Leaving social work when I became a mother, I began to focus on my new role. I believed that I could create happiness and love in my own family; I wanted to prove to myself that it was possible.

Being A Parent

On every child's face I see so much beauty, which reflects the angelic radiance of light and love. A parent's heart melts to see her baby mirroring this pristine purity and innocence. Almost every parent has a story of love at the first sight of his baby. My husband and I have ours. I remember an incident when my son was only three weeks old, not yet able to smile because his facial muscles were not yet developed to enable a smile. One night, in the dim nursery, as I rocked him, he looked intently at me with so much love. Then a smile on his face came from his soul. He seemed to be saying, "Mom, I am here!" My husband had a similar experience. When our baby was six months old, after his immunization shots earlier that day, he was running a low-grade fever. My husband showed his concern. Our little boy smiled and patted his father's face, as if he was saying, "Dad, don't worry. I am okay."

We fell in love with our baby. The joy of watching him grow and get active gave us immeasurable joy. We loved playing with him. We must admit, however, that sometimes the day-to-day care could be demanding and intense, especially when our child was young. Because our life revolved around his needs, we had little time for ourselves. Yet we felt so blessed to have him.

As cute as a baby or toddler is, a child's developmental needs and interests change. The cuteness of a toddler is not the same as that of a school-age child or a teenager. Parents also change, as do life circumstances. A family moves to another place, sometimes marriage falls apart, a member gets seriously ill, or a job changes. Life is always in a state of flux that challenges the parents to respond thoughtfully. For example, the ways we communicate with a preschooler would not be the same as with a school-age child. With each other, parents use more complex language to communicate, and our expectations are different. The family walks through many life stages with different problems that call for different solutions. Developmental and life changes ask us parents to respond to many things at once, to be like a conductor of a symphony. Keeping pace is mind-boggling. One thing I know for sure, though, is that, even with many life changes, pure love never changes.

One enigma about my child aroused great curiosity in me. Where did he come from? Did he have a soul? What would be the meaning of his life? My mother could not tell me what the meaning of life was. I could not tell him, either, because he had to find his own. What could we parents best give him, and how? Had my son and my husband and I known each other before in past lives? He seemed very familiar to us and we to him. When he was about two months old, I asked him one

22

day where he had been. As if he had heard me, he started babbling and gesturing with his hands to tell me his story. I listened, totally impressed with his effort to communicate with me. As I nodded, I had no clue what he was telling me. But this experience left me with the awe of his great soul. I wondered if other parents saw their children as human beings with souls.

And, so, we began our precious journey as a family. We held each other's hands and shared our love. We parents were caregivers and teachers, but our son was also our teacher. He opened my deep desire to find my own lost inner child, who was hidden underneath a pile of anger.

My Lost Inner Child

Underneath the pile of anger and confusion about what love was, I had to find my treasures: my diamond and inner music. These treasures would allow me to love myself again and to genuinely give to others from my heart. With limited self-love, I would end up repeating the same old pattern of conditional love that I had learned growing up. I would react rather than mindfully act. Sometimes in the dark of night, my soul called to me to find this lost angel.

I once wrote down my thoughts about the difference between being a spirited child and a lost child:

"A spirited child is one whose soul shines like a diamond in the sunshine. She is full of inner light and joyfulness. Her happiness touches the hearts of others. Her movements are like dancing and her voice is like a song. Her eyes sparkle. Her face beams with pure innocence.

On the contrary, a lost child is one who is enveloped in darkness and absorbed by anger. She doesn't trust people around her; she distrusts herself. Others don't care much about her. Emotionally abandoned, she creates her own safe world, where people would love her. She fantasizes to keep her hopes and dreams alive. The once beautiful and spirited child is deeply buried inside. She eventually becomes a stranger to herself."

I had to find my lost self. Once upon a time, the frightening noises of war and experiences with poverty had haunted my mother, blocking out joys in her life. Once upon a time, the noises in my own environment drowned the music inside me. The dust from living covered my diamond. Every child, including myself, needs love on earth. The anger in me gathered like clusters of broken leaves floating on the water's surface, blocking out sunlight. But the water underneath was still crystal clear.

I took a less traveled road, hoping to clear debris on the surface.

I wanted to hear my inner music and shine my diamond again. My intuition told me that to love others, I must reach inward to love myself. Carl Jung eloquently wrote, "Your vision will become clear only when you look into your heart; who looks outside dreams; who looks inside awakens."

3. MY BEGINNING:
A BLESSING OR A CURSE?

~

My mother loved telling two birth stories about me. One was that I was almost born breached. A British doctor in Hong Kong handily twisted me around. This might explain why I looked at the world so differently. The second story was that the nurse handed her the wrong baby. My mother's quick maternal instinct told her the baby wasn't me. Because I believe that I have lived in other lifetimes, I might have been a reluctant traveler to earth again.

My destiny was sealed. I became the second daughter, with an older sister and later a younger brother. My parents were both teachers in Hong Kong, where they lived after leaving Communist China in the late 1940s. My father taught science in a Catholic high school, while my mother taught grade school. We were part of an emerging middle class. We lived in a small flat but always had enough. We girls had a nanny who was a distant relative of my father and was also a new arrival in Hong Kong. She had tiny bound feet. I remember running her to exhaustion as she chased after me.

I was an active child, full of energy and happiness, as if the Inner

Light was still in me. I felt so joyful and silly that I sometimes made my serious mother laugh. Since toys were sparse, I found my own play, including jumping on a mattress like a trampoline with a friend until our parents yelled at us. Yet, underneath the joyfulness, I was a very sensitive and observing child, as if I was studying the world through my lenses. I would carefully listen to adult conversations and closely watch their interactions. Once in a while, even as young as four years old, I noticed someone acting oddly. What an adult person said and what she did made no sense to me. For instance, I overheard a friend of my parents criticizing a person when that person, usually a child, was standing right there. It was as if that child could not hear or feel, and the adult was unaware. Sometimes I was that criticized child. Little did I know, then, that this personal attribute of high sensitivity would be a blessing or a curse at various points in my life.

My carefree life ended when I was five. We emigrated to America, to the melting pot of New York City. In the late 1950s, the American government sent an immigration quota to Hong Kong to invite educated professionals and their families to come to America. In one of the best universities in China, my father had studied biological science. He was looking for better opportunities for himself and his family when he heard about this quota. He applied for immigration and got approved.

He came alone to New York City and settled in before his family joined him, eighteen months later.

My father found work as a medical researcher at a hospital, specializing in a then-new technology called the electron microscope. He also rented a small but comfortable apartment to welcome us to New York.

I remember the plane flight from Hong Kong to New York City. Just before we left, my mother had made new clothing for my doll, which my father had sent from America. At the airport, I held tightly onto my special doll in one hand and, in the other, a bag of sweets, which friends of my mother had given me. To my five-year-old self, they were my most prized possessions. Friends and relatives crowded the airport to say goodbye to us. My mother held her prized possessions all in one suitcase: photos, new clothing and some heirlooms. My sister had her doll. Our first stop was in Japan. My mother told me to leave my bag of sweets in the seat but I carried my doll. When I returned to the plane, I was so happy that my bag of sweets was still there. Landing in Honolulu, I left my bag of sweets in the plane, just like before. However, when I returned, we were on a different plane. I cried at the loss of my precious candies. That was my first trauma. The second was that my mother, my sister and I all had different seats. Both my sister and I cried until some kind passengers let us sit together. The trip to America was about separation from the familiar and a journey into the unknown and losing things along the way. It was obviously stressful for my sister and me, while my mother said that she had been nervous about missing the connecting flights. We all survived.

Right away, my parents settled us girls into a parochial school. Because we were just entering early grades, we adjusted with no difficulty. My parents had many friends who were also immigrants and who helped one another. A baby brother joined the family two years later.

However, the struggle to adapt was much harder for my mother. Her teaching experience was useless in America without knowing English. She had to take a menial job as a seamstress. Along with other Chinese-American mothers, she worked hard to raise her children, help make ends meet and keep the family together by maintaining cultural traditions. Now without a nanny, my mother had to juggle all her tasks. Without knowing English, she depended on my father and her children to interpret for her and to lead her around outside the Chinese community. Her dream of becoming a stylish career woman of the '50s vanished in the hardships of becoming an American.

During the 1950s in Hong Kong, my mother was an intelligent and beautiful woman. She always had her hair nicely done and wore stylish traditional dresses called *cheung-sam*. She enjoyed reading and writing. She once told me that one of her proudest moment was receiving her Hong Kong teaching certificate. When she married my father, who came from a long lineage of statesmen and scholars, she moved into a higher social circle. They had many friends. Now, as an immigrant, her status was low. In the face of so many challenges, she felt overwhelmed and powerless.

However, the birth of my brother, her American-born son, lifted her spirits. He became the main focus of her love. Males in traditional China were highly valued for prestige and status. Being a mother of one or more sons reflected a woman's highest achievement. Chinese families carried this value to America. Within my parents' social circle, mothers of sons in particular bragged about their sons fiercely, competing against each other for prestige and status. For example, my mother and another family friend both had sons almost the same age. I overheard their conversations bragging about whose son was more handsome and smart. The girls seemed secondary.

Lisa See, author of *Snow Flower and the Secret Fan*[1], described how the heroine in her story was harshly criticized by her mother in childhood. Chinese mothers used excessive criticism to prepare their daughters for the harsh married life ahead. Mothers passed on this practice from generation to generation for hundreds of years. The traditional Chinese culture regarded daughters as belonging to the future husband's family. But their in-laws still considered the brides as outsiders until they bore sons.

Growing up, my sister and I observed how our mother treated my brother differently. My parents' friends also treated boys differently from girls. My brother always got more. For instance, at Chinese New Year, in a good year, we kids could make over $100 when family friends gave money in red envelops. My younger brother always received more money than his sisters. At Christmas, he had more gifts. While the girls were assigned household chores, he, being a lot younger, had few. After a while, we girls accepted this practice and moved on to our own interests.

Underneath her pride in having a son, my mother became more and more depressed. The source was her difficult childhood. She told me that her mother had a very bad temper and yelled a lot. She didn't feel any love from her mother and her father, who sent money home from America, was simply absent.

My relationship with my father hung on a lighter note. When he became an American citizen, I was thrilled. Under the American citizenship law, his children automatically became "naturalized citizens."

As a nine year old, I could hardly wait to vote when I would come of age. Although growing up I was not close to him, we had some good times together. I remember enjoying being with him one-to-one when he took me to the mandatory church attendance on Sundays and to my weekly visit to the orthodontist. One Christmas, he surprised me with a large talk-and-walk doll. It wasn't until his old age that I felt closer to him, when I helped him to take care of mom and eventually took care of him after my mother's passing.

My father was not critical of the girls as my mother was, because he had a different perspective. Coming from a long line of well-to-do and educated people, he grew up in a large extended family. But, during the Japanese invasion and World War II, his family scattered. His mother worked to support her children, while his father went to another to city to do business. My father's older sister had a successful career as a nurse. Having also taught science in an all-girls' high school in Hong Kong, my father's view seemed to be that women were capable.

I loved my family of origin, but I had difficulty understanding them. Because I was so sensitive and observant, I was deeply affected by the shifting and sometimes dark moods in my family. My sensitivity worked against me; I felt darkness around me. Being the second daughter in a culture of rigid roles and power positions, I held the lowest rank in the family. They respected me only as a caregiver. At this time, my own negative tape spoke to me: "You can't do anything right, no matter how hard you try!"

From a young age, I could see through people's pretenses and intentions. Frequently, what they said and how they acted conflicted. I saw their inner feelings, as if I could read their hearts. For example, my mother's unhappiness hung over me like a dark drape.

My grade school friends served as outlets from my emotional alienation at home. However, I was afraid of the nuns and priests. In the name of God, they held the power to control and scare us. What I saw underneath, though, was that they were just people. Being able to see through others' pretenses was confusing for me, because I did not understand what those perceptions meant.

Some of the darkness lifted when I entered high school. After my grade school graduation, we moved from New York City to Boston. My father had a new job in Boston. A change in the environment helped me to emotionally distance myself from the family's moods. Studies, friends and social activities occupied my time. Surprisingly, my relationship with my mother improved, because I was less dependent on her. We had more to share, as if we were sisters. Although I didn't hear the negative tape as loudly, then, it was always playing inside my head.

A Lull

In college I began putting my best foot forward. I majored in child development/family relations and psychology, which enabled me to hone my observational skills. I loved learning, and had a good sense of people. After undergraduate school, I went on to earn my Masters in social work, training to do psychotherapy, particularly family therapy. My sensitivity gave me an edge in clinical assessment as I could probe into people's moods. My perceptiveness in seeing through people's pretenses provided me better understanding of their problems. Insightful assessment helped me to apply more effective therapeutic techniques.

In Boston, I worked at child welfare agencies in different capacities, including as a supervisor and program director. While I was building self-confidence in my profession, I was also building a mental picture of the kind of family I wanted. For sure, I wished to end the legacy of my childhood past—not only the favoring of males in the family but also the thoughtless and conflicting communication, of what people said and what they actually did in contradiction. I believed in a strong marital relationship and good communication with children.

Then I met my husband. At the agency where I was working, the new director invited an independent research consultant to evaluate one of the programs. I knew that her strategy would be to fire old staff if the consultant documented a poor program. Since I was coordinating the agency's volunteer training program, I met with this consultant. He was a handsome, blond-haired, soft-spoken guy. It was love at first sight. Not only was the program evaluation positive but also, some months later, we were married.

My husband and I couldn't have been more different in our backgrounds. He was of Scottish descent and grew up in white, middle-class suburbia—what I call the "Dick and Jane" world. My first encounter with American suburbia was in that beginner's reading series when I was in first grade. That world was incomprehensible to me: a place where all the characters were happy and playful. They lived in houses with backyards. They rode wagons and had dogs romping around. My own urban world was a far cry from Dick and Jane. In the city, we lived in apartments and learned to walk fast for safety. The only backyard I knew was the playground behind my school. But both my husband and I believed that these background differences were not significant and served to enrich our lives. Our hearts were one.

My parents welcomed my husband into the family. My mother loved having another son, her second son-in-law. My sister had married a wonderful man of French-Canadian descent. My mother's fine Chinese cooking helped bring this melting pot family together.

My father-in-law was a gentle and easy-going person whose parents had come from Glasgow, Scotland, at the beginning of the twentieth century. When the shipbuilding business in Glasgow declined, his father, my husband's grandfather, found better opportunities in a shipyard in Quincy, Massachusetts. With his parents coming from Scotland, my father-in-law understood the immigrant experience. My mother-in-law called herself a Yankee. Her father had also worked in the Quincy shipyard. She traced her father's ancestors back to the *Mayflower*, although her mother's side was Scottish from Nova Scotia, Canada.

Several years later, our son was born, blending the East and West. His smiles and happiness lighted our lives and blurred the cultural dividing lines, at least for a while. I decided to be a full-time mother. I was grateful to have this choice: simply to be there for my child and not to miss any of his milestones. I wanted to build a loving family.

As happy as I was with a new baby and a supportive husband, I was still unhappy within myself. I still suppressed my anger from long ago. Moreover, I thought much about God and my soul. Feeling displaced— separate and disconnected from my soul, I desired deep truths, but had no idea where to begin looking for them. I needed time to reflect and do soul-searching.

One happy outcome of being a new mother was that I finally bridged the rift between my mother and me. We bonded as mothers. However, she still believed in male favoritism and still suffered from her depression. In retrospect, my mother loved us all. Her traditional values and painful childhood experiences just made it difficult for her to express her love to her daughters. In the end, the person she loved least was herself.

While I was relishing the joys of motherhood, something else was brewing in the background. The old negative voice, my cursed sensitivity, said, "You can't do anything right, no matter how hard you try." It gradually spoke louder and louder, finally pounding my mind and heart into a wave of anxiety.

4. IN THE LAND OF OLD AND NEW MOTHERS

~

Being a mother suddenly transported me to the land of old and new mothers. Mothering is not a neutral territory; it has many experts and many more opinions. There are at least three voices: your own, your mother's, and your mother-in-law's. The lucky ones hear one unified voice; the unlucky ones may hear three conflicting voices. I heard two—my own and my mother-in-law's.

When I was first married, I thought that I had a good rapport with my mother-in-law. I was open to a new perspective on mainstream American life. She lived everything that was American, from flying the American flag in front of her house on Independence Day to the careful preservation of family heritage. In her living room, the oil portrait of a Scottish great-grandfather in the 1800's watched over the grandfather clock, both which had to be perfectly lined up with the antique chair. In contrast, my parents had brought with them a few treasures that fit into one suitcase.

My in-laws were doting grandparents. They had fun taking care of and playing with their grandson. Like Santa Claus, Papa made lots of wooden toys in his workshop and Grammy painted them. They celebrated holidays with all the excitement of American traditions. My little boy loved them. My mother-in-law was a respectable member of her community where she had lived all her life. She had a Master's degree in American history. She served in several historical societies.

But my mother-in-law also took on an unspoken role as the one to instill her heritage in her half-Caucasian grandson. She wanted him to experience her Dick and Jane world of the '50s, where children played in yards and roamed in neighbors' houses. In her south of Boston suburbia at that time, it was possible for her son and his friends to play freely in the neighborhood. However, her Dick and Jane world did not exist for me. I grew up in New York City where neighbors did not have their doors unlocked for kids to walk in and play. Living in a small apartment, I did not have a backyard. Our mothers worked. Safe playing on the streets was a concern for me.

In the changing world of the 1980s, I was not convinced that playing in backyards with neighborhood children was the only method of socialization. I took an eclectic approach, doing what I thought was appropriate and not necessarily playing by Dick-and-Jane rules. Unfortunately, I couldn't talk to my mother-in-law about cultural differences and today's lifestyle. Within the family, my mother-in-law had a hidden rule: we could only chitchat. Heartfelt communication was sparse.

She never openly criticized my mothering behaviors, yet I clearly felt her disapproval and judgment of me. To me, "what she said" and "what she really meant" were often at odds. She rarely said any direct disapproving words to me, but all that remained unsaid—tones, gestures and actions—told another story. What was left unsaid was open to interpretation and left me feeling her disapproval. I was not seeking her approval as much as I wanted to be congenial with her. But my old negative tape was shouting at me again. I became anxious and stressed out. I sometimes lost my temper with my young son, only to feel bad afterward.

To keep peace, my husband and I went along with the chitchatting at family gatherings. To broaden our experiences beyond one community, we took our son to other nearby communities to do fun things. He enjoyed playing with children of different backgrounds, going to music classes, attending reading and social programs. We as a family also developed a passion to travel. At age five, our son was enthralled on his first trip abroad to London. All in all, he felt only love and happiness from everyone.

Nonetheless, my high sensitivity and ability to see through people's pretenses worked against me. I absorbed the negative energies in my environment. From time to time, I also glimpsed my vulnerability: who was I, really?

A big change came when my husband got a job in San Francisco. But when we moved from Massachusetts to California, I packed up my depression, anxiety and negative tape and brought them with me.

Escape to the Land of Tiger Moms

My son entered first grade in the local public school in a suburb south of Berkeley. I understood that many mothers worked or had to work, but I decided to continue being a full- time mother. Having experience working with children, I volunteered at my son's school. I quickly made friends with a few mothers. In general, I stepped into a new territory that I called the "Land of Tiger Moms."

The "Tiger Mom" phenomenon refers to the aggressive ways that mothers push their children to achieve academic excellence. In traditional Chinese culture, becoming a scholar was the only way to get out of poverty or to move up the social and economic ladder. It also would bring honor to the family's name. Chinese families have carried this same value to America, the land of many opportunities. Asian children in general are expected to excel in school. Over the decades, Asian parents have fine-tuned their skills to get their children to top colleges. They know what their children have to do to get to the top. The pressure is on to do all the right things, each step of the way, beginning with kindergarten.

Today, Tiger Moms don't necessarily have Asian faces. They come from many ethnic and racial backgrounds. They play the same game of moving their children ahead to compete and outdo other children. The game is survival of the fittest. Being a classroom mother, I observe firsthand the games played, sometimes with negative impact on students' self-esteem.

First, I notice how some mothers flatter teachers so that their children will get more encouragement and favoritism. For young children who are just building their self-confidence as learners, a little favoritism or encouragement can go a long way. Stickers only provide so much positive reinforcement. I see the quiet confusion and sad faces on those students who get less attention. Moreover, the labeling process within the school system also sorts out gifted and average students through standardized test scores. In my mind, the statistical bell curve leaves lots of students in the middle who can do better or worse depending on how they are treated. This sorting out process reminds me of separating good apples from bad ones before they are ripe.

I have another observation: we mothers don't really know what we are doing. I notice mothers metaphorically looking over other mothers' shoulders to learn what to do. If my child is doing what other children are doing, there is safety in numbers. We can't go wrong. The pressure is on all mothers to have their children do almost the same thing. For example, in the '90s, the *Goosebumps* book series was very popular. Almost every child held those books in their hands, while their mothers beamed with pride. (This was before Harry Potter days.) But my then nine-year-old son wouldn't read them or any similar series. He said, "They are dumb books." He would rather watch PBS or science programs on television. One day, his clever father suggested *Jurassic Park* by Michael Crichton. Our son loved it and afterward read many more science fiction books.

The Tiger Mom style of parenting looks like a cookie-cutter style to me. Everyone has to do the same thing, whatever it is, but the competition among mothers is fierce. If you are smarter parent, you can do it better. And the ultimate prize of having your child go to a prestigious college or be an all-star athlete reflects your accomplishment as a parent.

As for me as an elementary-school mother, I had two problems. One, my sensitivity and perceptiveness drew me a different kind of parenting for a school-age child. Our children need love more than they need to learn the game of getting ahead. I felt the pressure to follow the crowd, and, at the same time, I also questioned what were the right things to do. Another problem was my son. Not only was he bright, he also had a mind of his own. Even if I had tried to play the Tiger Mom game, he wouldn't let me. He had other ideas, but I wasn't listening to him as I should have.

By the end of my son's fifth grade, I burned-out as a school volunteer, getting tired of school politics and the games mothers played with each other. From sixth grade to high school, my son attended a private college-preparatory school.

A Curse Becomes A Gift

Leaving the world of school volunteerism, I finally turned inward, asking myself what were the things that I was doing wrong? I was never good enough in meeting others' rules and requirements. Who made those right-and-wrong rules, which could change from society to society, or person to person? What my mother would say was right; what my mother-in-law would say was wrong. To whom should I listen? Moreover, the right-and-wrong rules appeared to be intended to control and not to foster love. If I was so wrong, why was there so much love within my own family?

Is the Tiger Mom method the only good way of parenting? Does climbing the Ivy League towers and the corporate ladder really prepare our children to face life's many challenges: losses, illnesses, failures, divorce or death? How can we give them the tools to handle those situations? How can we better communicate with them? How can we help them to build strong character or to make good judgments? How can we teach them to show compassion and to develop meaningful relationships? This nonacademic aspect of parenting is an integral and vital part of good parenting.

All children have different needs and different personalities. We parents also don't know their life purposes. Clearly, one size—that is, one way of parenting—does not fit all. We parents play a guessing game, plotting what we see as the best path and hoping for the best. Certainly, it is our responsibility as parents to nurture them, keep them safe and guide them. We provide opportunities for a good education and preparation for the future. Most importantly, we give children our love. Should this love be the kind our parents and society gave us when we grew up, or is it something else?

By that point, I had trod the landscape of doing or not doing the right things that I was told. I had been lost for decades amid too many conflicting messages and too much harshness. When my old negative tape wasn't shouting at me, I could still feel its vibration. I saw how people played mind games, sometimes thoughtlessly hurting one another. The mind games were often words said and actions taken for personal convenience or gain, with little awareness of their impact on others. We may say or do things to get others off our backs, to get ahead, or to appear important. We may say one thing and then do something else.

For example, to stop my son from fussing, I would promise him a toy. To a child at age two, this promise would work as a distraction, and I would not have to follow through and actually give him a toy. But as he grew, he remembered such promises when I made them and reminded me. From my professional and personal experiences with children, I learned that they don't forget such promises. Even if they feel they can't remind their parents of them, they keep a list of broken promises in their hearts, as well as the hurt they caused.

Everything one says or does matters. A fundamental law of physics states that every action has a reaction. Over time, actions and reactions have significant impact.

My inner landscape looked distorted and bleak. There was too much darkness and not enough light; there was too much fear and not enough love. But I owned my feelings and perceptions. I was experiencing my life through my own lenses—turned upside down, metaphorically speaking, as if I were still a breach baby. I was responsible for the position I was in. It was my love for my husband and son, and their love for me, that held me together. We had a warm family where we felt safe and had the freedom to be who we were. I wanted to be a happier person, with inner peace for myself and for them. I needed to clean out the skeletons from my closet and to find a higher perspective on life.

I embarked on a quest for deeper understanding. The desire to heal my emotional alienation, along with my desire to see a more peaceful and loving world, propelled me to follow my inner path. Moreover, my longing for God grew stronger and stronger, even though I didn't know if God existed. I wanted Heaven to give me some answers and began my quest to find them. I started to pray and turned my soul toward the Light.

A Glimpse of Inner Light

When I was quiet enough, I started hearing an occasional whisper, not actual sounds but a flutter of vibration in very high frequencies. It reminded me of an invisible hummingbird flapping its wings. I thought it was my imagination. But when my mind was quiet, I could hear clear messages. For example, I had been very annoyed with a mother who bragged about how her brilliant son fluently spoke two languages. (Her son was my son's friend.) A beautiful voice from within me said, "Sit down and listen. This mother was proud of her family's unique overseas experiences." The voice asked me to let her remark go. Who was speaking to me?

One Saturday afternoon, while my son and husband were away overnight for a Boy Scouts outing, I mindlessly turned on the television, which happened to be on PBS. Two authors, Barbara Mark and Trudy Griswold, were speaking on communication with angels. With lessons from their new book called *The Angelspeake Book of Prayer and Healing*[2], they taught the audience to do automatic writing of messages from angels. They also cautioned the audience to pray first for divine protection, so that the communication would be pure.

I tried my first automatic writing with a prayer for divine protection. I asked who this beautiful voice speaking to me was. Here are a few early entries:

"Dear Beloved. My name is Omega, your guardian angel. I am an angel of Grace who is helping you to reach

God. We angels are the Essence of God's love. We extend His Love to you. When you feel the storm around you, feel the pillar of our strength and calmness. We care about you."

"Love is an important theme in your life. Many times when you sought love in the world, you found naught. Your feelings were left empty. Be one with us Spirits. We lift you with our love and joy. Stay close to us."

Omega used "we" to connote the presence of more than one angel or spirit. Her voice was in unity with One Spirit.

How could I tell if I was making up the messages? Mark and Griswold spoke of "shivers running down the spine." Shivers in my spine and disbelief were indeed what I experienced. Despite being skeptical of what I was hearing, I was also drawn with great curiosity to this Inner Light. I couldn't shut out this wonderful experience. What if angels were real? Through prayers and meditation, I learned to listen quietly to whispers that revealed timeless wisdom. I couldn't possibly invent them, because they were lifting me up with so much love, not beating me down, as I was doing to myself. Something special was coming to me from the Divine World. My heart and mind were opening, like a lotus flower beginning to bloom.

Omega and many more wonderful Spirit Friends came, not to change my outer landscape, but to heal my inner core. Omega and Spirit Friends taught me how to listen to my inner voice and to turn my curse—high sensitivity and perceptiveness—into a psychic gift. Their gift to me was the beginning of a spiritual awakening.

5. GREGORY: A SPECIAL TEACHER

~

Divine Spirits have always been with me in different ways in different periods of my life. Their invisible presence has comforted and guided me. At times, their loving touch feels like a pink blanket wrapping around me; at times, their messages of guidance show me the way.

Before age six, I was aware of a protective Light with me. I was a happy child, full of laughter and joy. This joy waned when I reached school age. However, once in a while, beginning at age nine, I could sense a unique presence whose name began with "G." I wondered if it was Archangel Gabriel, whom I read about in catechism, or some other spirit who loved me. At age fourteen, in the middle of the night, while in a semi-awakened state, I heard a voice from within that I clearly knew was not my own. It said, "Jesus loves you. You are very compassionate." This voice deeply impressed my young heart, reminding me that I was more than what I thought I was.

As I grew up, Jesus never spoke to me through any organized religions in which I participated. My parents never discussed religion at home, even though they were active members of the Catholic Church. At the parochial school that I attended, I dreaded confession and speaking to the mystery man inside the confessional. In those days, we children were told that we were sinful and had to go to confession before receiving the Holy Eucharist. I never knew how many "Our Father" and "Hail Mary" prayers other kids had to say for punishment, but to my young mind the number of these prayers that the mysterious priest inside the confessional gave me indicated the severity of my sins. For a bad confession, my punishment would be five or more of each prayer. The lighter penalty would be two or three of each, but I never got away without penalty or with any blessings that I could remember. So, I was greatly relieved when confessions and required mass attendance ended upon eighth-grade graduation. Those experiences never told me of a loving God, just a punitive one.

At the end of high school and beginning of college, I attended an evangelical church for three years. While I liked reading the Bible, I was not convinced of God's love from the fiery sermons. In that church I felt as if I were an outcast, because I didn't think I needed to be a born-again Christian. I loved Jesus already and I didn't understand what made me so sinful. I took my love for the Bible and church music with me, but I never again participated in any organized religion.

In my twenties, I began an intellectual search for God through studying religions. I read about Buddhism, Hinduism and other religious philosophies. All major religions held the same highest truth about God. There was one God who was above religions. However, my mind did not understand Him because my heart was not fully open. Religious studies could not show me the way to God. But the Divine Spirits understood my dilemma and directly reached out to me. They communicated with me through life experiences.

For example, one time when I was in a college bookstore, I saw a poster that immediately grabbed my attention. It said, "It is only with the heart that one sees clearly. What is essential is invisible to the eyes." This revealing quote came from the book *The Little Prince* by Antoine de St. Exupéry.[3] I bought this poster and hung it above my bed in my dorm. These words touched my heart, speaking a deep truth that I somehow had already known. At that time, many young people my age were relentlessly competing with each other and seeking material success, so much so that they forgot what was inside their hearts.

I also had the strong intuition that I needed to connect with God, who could help me to navigate my life. He was my directional Source to guide me on the highway with no signs. But where and who was God? Intellectually I didn't know who God was, but in my heart I did, although I was not consciously aware of this. I am reminded of an anonymous saying, "When you are seeking something, that something is already seeking you." God was already seeking me.

When I was a young mother, I had some mystical experiences. For example, one day, I saw Brilliant Light enveloping me on a sunny summer day while I was in the backyard, as Heaven's love and joy opened to me for few seconds. I said to myself, "Did I make this up?" Sometimes, I smelled the fragrance of fresh flowers from nowhere. I also had other moments of clarity and divine touches—a loving inner voice calling me, a flash of vision or an inner knowing—which were always accompanied by feelings of omnipotent love streaming from Heaven to remind me of joy.

Becoming A Student

Starting in the early nineties, while taking care of my family after moving to California, I wanted to heal my depression and anger. I wanted more Light on my path to combat the darkness in my life. The time had come to take a quantum leap into spiritual awakening and to listen to the intuition in my heart.

Besides my guardian angel, Omega, other Divine Spirits communicated in unison with no distinctive personalities, just one voice and one love. They were Highly Evolved Spirits who had lived on earth. They knew me well and spoke loving words. I called them Blessed Spirits.

Their words sounded like music when I listened to them. Also, an imagery of their words looked like many gentle snowflakes falling from Heaven. As more snow fell, the landscape began to change, creating a new essence of its own. I made angel wings on the snow because I wanted, like them, to be loving and wise. A whole new world was opening to me.

When I reached my hands upward, Heaven reached back down to me. In unison, angels and Divine Spirits spoke, **"No problem or request is too small for us. Ask and believe that your prayers are answered. Open your heart and mind to our love. We love you. Trust us. We are real."**

All messages were from One Source—God, and this One Voice was not from my own random thinking, because my mind was too cluttered with worries and negativity. The Voice was consistent and powerful in my reality. It quietly cracked through the surface of my rambling thoughts when I was not actively thinking about anything. It came between thoughts, into gaps of silence, when I was driving, doing chores, or meditating.

There is a Higher Dimension always surrounding us, which we

cannot see or hear. Yet, in moments of grace, when we seek Divinity, Heaven readily speaks to us. I imagine my mind to be like a ham radio, transmitting electromagnetic waves back and forth with an outside source. The clarity of the Inner Voice depends upon the person's state of mind and emotions, similar to the sound waves going through a filter. The less cluttered the mind and the calmer the emotions, the clearer the sound is. I could telepathically sort out the varying frequencies of tones and pick up messages.

To me, angels were overwhelmingly affectionate and gentle. They lifted my spirit. These "Blessed Spirits" were very wise and kind, helping me with healing. Slowly, I began to awake from within.

In the early years of spiritual awakening, Divine Spirits wanted to fill me with the overflowing unconditional love that was lacking in my life. One day, I had an unusual conversation with my then seven-year-old son. As we were driving past an automobile repair shop, we played a game of pretending to be cars and talked about what our cars needed. When it came to my car, he astutely remarked, "Mom, you want to run on Super Unleaded gasoline, but your engine can't handle it!" I was surprised by his comment. Yes, I wanted to change the world, but I didn't feel that I had enough inside me to accomplish much.

Angels and Blessed Spirits poured unconditional love into me to break up my negative energies. No matter how much I complained about my worries and anxieties, they were always patient with me. I felt overflowing love lifting my spirit, sometimes for a few minutes, other times seeping into the long memory of my heart. The unconditional love from Heaven filled me like Super Unleaded gasoline; only they also fixed my engine so I could handle it!

Blessed Spirits shared another wisdom with me. They showed me that my hypersensitivity had two sides: one that I had used against myself, and the other one that I could use to assist myself. Society defines hypersensitivity as a negative trait in which the individual is prone to personal hurt. Oftentimes I took people's abrasive remarks or rude behaviors personally. However, Divine Spirits revealed to me that my hypersensitivity really reflected my ability to pick up other people's subtle energies. I had a psychic gift of hearing people's hearts, and sometimes reading their minds. Therefore, I could see through people's pretenses. Divine Spirits told me how to "tune into my own heart" and "to tune out other people's negativity." For example, when someone speaks abrasive words to me, she is saying something about what is going on inside her. I sense her inner message. My wise response often is to walk away.

As my spirit grew stronger, the voices of Blessed Spirits played a more important role in my spiritual learning. They were my personal teachers for my individualized curriculum. My education included not only taking notes and reading books that grabbed my attention at the library or bookstores, but also experiencing hands-on practice in my everyday life. Like a good student, I applied my learning. The training was rigorous and humbling, because Blessed Spirits understood my strengths and weaknesses and what I needed to learn.

Over a period of weeks, for example, I kept seeing mental images of fire. But I had no idea of its meaning, nor did I ask. One Sunday morning, my son saw the standing halogen lamp in the family room blinking without anyone touching it. My husband went over to check it and found that the heat from the halogen bulb had burned through the inner metal shade. He immediately threw out the lamp. On the same day, I spotted an article in the newspaper about the serious fire hazards of halogen lamps. It appeared that the Divine Spirits had repeatedly warned me of a fire hazard, but I didn't understand the message. Then they used the electricity of a blinking light to get our attention. And was the news article that I read on the same day a coincidence? I doubted it. From then on, I paid more attention to mental images through my Third Eye and listened closely to my intuition.

There is a saying that "a teacher arrives when the student is ready." I was ready and eager for more learning.

Gregory, My Spirit Teacher

Among this group of Blessed Spirits, one distinct Divine Spirit came into my awareness. I recognized his very high frequency that emits very fast but subtle vibration, which I can feel through my sixth sense. One morning, while driving home after dropping my son off at his high school, I noticed a brilliant light surrounding me. I saw a tint of golden light enveloping the interior of my car, as if someone had turned up the voltage of a powerful light bulb. Doubting my own eyes, I ignored this presence, but its energy was too high. The deep baritone vibration sounded masculine, as opposed to the feminine presences of a higher vibrational frequency that I'd heard.

Without asking who he was and with great annoyance, I asked why he was so happy. He answered, **"Why aren't you?"** I gave a featherbrained answer that it was not my style and sighed heavily. In fact, I often felt troubled by the thoughtless and mean ways people treated one another, showing little regard for each other's feelings or the consequences of their words and actions. I felt the weight of the world on my shoulders. Dismissing this spirit as being just my imagination, I shifted back to the real world of driving and endless worries, ignoring this high-energy, happy spirit.

Fortunately, this Blessed Spirit had better sense than I did. He bypassed my mental block by contacting a friend whose daughter was a grade-school classmate of my son. We met through being room-mothers. As we worked in our children's third-grade classroom, we had many opportunities to talk. What bought us close together was the mutual discovery of our psychic gifts. We both had the ability to communicate with Divine Spirits, who sometimes spoke to both of us at the same time! Our friendship continued after our children went to different schools. I had not spoken within her for several weeks, and she did not know of my recent distress over human behaviors. The following day, she called me up and said, "While I was meditating, I got a message for you. He tells you to lighten up." I was stunned. Who was he?

As I meditated on his powerful presence, whose love I felt deeply, I saw an image of a spirit dancing joyfully. He was full of energy and zeal. I gave him a random name, Gregory, because he reminded me of the strong spirit presence that began with the initial "G" that I'd encountered when I was nine years old. At that time, I had thought that the spirit presence was Archangel Gabriel. I could have given Gregory another name: George, Glen. However, the name Gregory strongly impressed itself on my mind. He became Gregory to me, and, through me, to the world.

One time, when I was standing by the Point Reyes Lighthouse in California, I saw shimmering sunlight reflecting and dancing on the ocean surface. My heart skipped a beat at the sight of such joyfulness. Gregory's voice said to me that his name in Chinese means "shimmering light on water," although he wasn't Chinese or of any definitive ethnicity; he gave a descriptive name in Chinese characters that clearly described his Light.

I wrote down one of Gregory's very early communications:

"I am close to Christ Light and am radiating Jesus' loving energy to you. Have no fear. Have hope, joy and love in your heart. Remember that you have always known me. I understand the religions of the East and West. I am here to help you integrate the various religions into one understanding, outside of any religions. We are all Divine Spirits. My high energy comes from my pure love for God."

His words inspired great curiosity in me. I wanted to know more about Gregory, my personal spirit teacher. I asked many questions: Who was he and why was he here? What was the nature of our relationship in the past, and did we have any past lives together? For sure, I recognized his high energy. When I was with Gregory, I forgot my own sadness. As happy as he seemed to me, he also had a serious, intellectual side along with a great sense of humor. Whenever I got upset about something, he would say, **"I am not laughing at you, but with you. Lighten up!"**

Early in our contact, I stayed up late one night, after the rest of the family had gone to bed. I inquired into Gregory's history. He revealed that he was an apostle of Jesus. He said, **"I was Simon, but not Simon Peter."** Right afterward, the light above my head blinked several times and I felt a chill all over me. (I checked to see if the bulb was loose; it was not.) This revelation caught me by surprise, because I did not remember all the names of Jesus' twelve apostles. I knew of Simon Peter as the first pope of the Catholic Church. With catechism well forgotten, I checked an old Bible for the apostles' names. There were indeed two Simons: Simon Peter and Simon the Zealot! So I was communicating with Simon the Zealot, who was full of the high energy: zeal! Amazing! He said,

"I was not among the central apostles that the Biblical writers remembered, but my love for Jesus equaled the other apostles. Among the twelve of us, each had a different role to

play according to his personality and calling. I played more of the peripheral role in the whole drama with Jesus' life. I dealt with authorities, particularly in the protection of Jesus when necessary. I played a supportive but passionate role. Jesus understood my devotion. His deep understanding of my love was sufficient for me. The quiet power of Jesus' eyes is what you see of my eyes in your mind."

I was flabbergasted and honored to be speaking an apostle. He answered, **"Everyone is famous in his or her own way. It is the way one touches others' lives. Some appear more famous by definition of your society, but not by God."** He continued,

"I learned from Jesus that the power of God's love was sufficient for me. I had lots of anger toward the Romans who oppressed the Jews. However, Jesus taught me that this anger got in the way of healing myself. I worked on my anger by not allowing it to dictate my actions. I learned to examine my choices and to choose wisely. Jesus said to me that actions stemming from love ultimately have the real power to heal and change. The energy of love can alter and shift negative energy into positive. The more love you

have inside, the more you can send out to others. I learned from Jesus that forgiving your enemies and doing good for them, when appropriate, is the best weapon—that is, using spiritual light."

Gregory shared with me that we'd had many lifetimes together. He pointed out several notable ones, two in Medieval Europe and one in China in the sixteenth century. In one medieval lifetime, he was an abbot, perhaps Abbot Gregory, and I was his student. In that lifetime, I wanted to understand why people were not seeking God for healing and help. I saw so much human suffering in which God could have an effect. Gregory told me that people saw themselves as being separated from God, despite the tremendous influence of the Catholic Church. The material world was their only reality. In another medieval time, he was a Franciscan friar who was briefly my spiritual advisor. As a noble woman, I was devoted to serving the poor and sick.

In our final past life together, in sixteenth-century China, Gregory played the role of my son to give me the courage to live through a difficult life as a woman in an oppressive Chinese society. As a daughter in a wealthy family, I was the social rebel who fought traditional matchmaking. In the end, I yielded to an arranged marriage. To keep my inner peace, I avoided the contentious household by devoting myself to a quiet religious life. As my son, Gregory became a monk, never caring for wealth or status. He told me that this lifetime in China was his last incarnation on earth. In my heart I knew that he made this last sacrifice to come to earth just for me. Our love was very deep and strong.

I can't know if any of these memories are real, because there is no proof. They might be real because I feel their reality in my heart. Examining my spiritual odyssey over the past few years, I know that my spiritual experiences have been coherent, unified and powerful—with no contradictions or discrepancies. Gregory and I seem to share the same passion for social justice. In several lifetimes we were together to accomplish shared missions. Besides our shared missions, we truly love each other. In each of those several lifetimes, our love has deepened. He said, **"Pure love between two persons magnifies when they walk the earth journey together."** What this means is that through the physical earth experience of pure love, the energy of love expands and strengthens. Only love is real.

Now Gregory is my spirit teacher who guides me on my path, but he never interferes with my life without my permission. **"Love just is this way: free, eternal and all encompassing,"** he told me. He hinted to me that he and I had work to do, when the time was right. Wonderful, I asked myself: what could I possibly do for anyone else when I still had so much to learn, myself? It would be like the blind leading the blind. But I sensed that Gregory was not concerned about my doubt and lack of insight. Something big was about to happen.

6. A GLOBAL SHIFT

~

In the late summer of 2001, just before my son's senior year in high school, he was hiking with his classmates in the Sierras for four weeks. This wilderness experience was part of his school's required curriculum for graduation. Now I had more quiet time to myself, but I felt restless. The outward tranquility did not reflect my sense of turbulence in the air. Gregory's energy got increasingly high. I was thinking a lot about how we parents were working hard to raise our children, but we still lacked certainty as to what are the right things to do.

The joys of parenting by far exceed the trials and challenges we face. The miracle of a newborn puts us in awe. The developmental milestones—the first steps, first words, first day of school, etc.—send parents running to their cameras to post pictures on the fridge and on Facebook. Children's laughter and playfulness let us forget our troubles; their innocence and joyfulness touch our deep desire to reclaim that forgotten happiness. Moreover, the love that they have for us and our love for them move us to be better people for them. These experiences of joy light our lives against the shadows of darker challenges.

One dark challenge appears to be those nebulous forces enveloping our lives that we cannot control. For instance, electronic devices such as the iPhone and Internet greatly enhance social connections and awareness of the world. However, they are also very addictive to young people, because they are symbols of entrance to adult world. Everyone is using them for fun and entertainment. Furthermore, violence in video games and movies can also subconsciously affect their perceptions about the world. Virtual violence, in my opinion, can numb the mind and senses to the reality of pain and suffering of others. Young people cannot escape these influences, nor can parents protect them.

CNN.com (10/02) did a survey on parenting, "Easier Said Than Done." It explored how confident parents were in instilling values in their children. The result showed that 61 percent of the respondents rated themselves "fair to poor" in communicating values to their children. Why aren't the parents confident in their communication? What are they saying to their children? Why aren't the children listening? How could we parents do better?

Divorce devastates and fractures many families, and after sudden illness or an accident families struggle to cope. Death leaves family members silent and isolated in their grief. Any kind of discrimination, prejudice and bullying also instills tremendous emotional suffering. The state of families is not peaceful; neither is the state of the world.

In the midst of my pondering, my son returned from his month long Sierra hike. He looked very tired, but at the same time possessed a new sense of confidence. He and his high school classmates had struggled hard together to live in the wilderness, through painful blisters on their feet, rain, heat, and rough mountain terrain. They'd had to compromise their differences and arguments to help each other. Moreover, he learned independence and self-reliance.

Early September, we were busy preparing for his senior year in high school. One afternoon, while I was doing the dishes, I heard an inner voice saying, **"You shall see deaths."** I saw a flashed vision of smoke and ashes. This voice assured me that my family was going to be safe. I was very puzzled.

The Shift: 9/11

On September 11th, 2001, at six in the morning West Coast time, my husband woke me. He said, "You ought to see this. Something big is happening." I was looking forward to sleeping later that morning, because my husband was going to drive our son to school and my van was in the repair shop. We couldn't believe the scene we were watching on television, the images moving quickly across the screen like virtual reality. The first plane hit and the second one followed; the twin towers collapsed, with smoke and ashes everywhere; people were screaming and scrambling in pandemonium. This location of the Twin Towers was not far from where I grew up. I suddenly remembered the premonition I'd had several weeks before. I felt a chill all over me.

Two days later, on the way to pick up my van, I walked three miles to the subway station. During this long walk, I asked Gregory for the meaning of this event. He told me that Heaven had seen it coming for a long time. Because people have free will to act, Heaven could not stop the violence. This event had been set in motion long ago, but right now this tragedy appeared to be an isolated event. It was not. He said,

"This tragedy has occurred. This event has set international affairs on a collision course, in which global tension will flare up in all parts of the world. It is a manifestation of longstanding historical tension, dating back hundreds if not thousands of years ago. The world is now at a stage for more rapid changes."

"So much has happened in the last few days that it is overwhelming to know where to begin or what to do. I see how this tragedy can tip people's spirits either way: to seek and do good, or to continue on the path of destruction. People are inwardly thinking, consciously or

subconsciously, how to make sense of this tragic event that took so many lives in an instant. The loud ones speak up and the quiet ones withdraw. To make sense of this tragedy is on everyone's mind; let us pray that people will choose good over evil, and peace over violence."

"It is truly a time for reflection, a time to stop and think about what really matters in your life. Is it money, wealth, status and power? Or is it something else? It is a time for individuals to look inward and find strengths that are needed to build peace."

"In your world of cause and effect, this tragedy cannot be undone. What can be undone is the mental pollution. Only people, as individuals and as groups, can stop further destruction. I am referring not only to the physical destruction, but also the rampant greed and violence in the minds and hearts of many people. Pray for the world to make wise choices in their thoughts, words and actions so to bring peace. This is a sober time for everyone."

What Gregory said surprised me. The destruction was horrendous, but apparently it did not happen out of the blue, as it appeared. Global tensions had been going on for a long time that most of us could not understand, nor were we aware of the political complexity. Terrorism springs from a group's sense of outrage, warranted or not. However, each of us has the responsibility to find solutions for peace in our lives, while political leaders do their work to protect citizens and bring global peace.

For certain, the September 11th tragedy has forever touched, changed and redefined the lives of many people at home and abroad. I felt the anguish and intense grief of families who lost their loved ones in the World Trade Center. The sudden nature and magnitude of losses would always be in their hearts and minds. How could we make sense of such a horrific event? How could we take this tragedy and turn it into something good? It would be like rising out of the rubble and creating a monument from ashes. How could we heal, or could we ever be healed? Where is the hope of peace for our children?

September 11th jolted our sleeping egos. Our old consciousness has changed. It tells us that we cannot continue living our lives the same way or seeing ourselves the same way. We can no longer hide our heads in the sand or look the other way, waiting and hoping for someone else to fix our problems. September 11th was a rude awakening.

I asked Gregory what could each of us do? How could one person bring peace and make a difference against this catastrophic destruction, which had sent ripples all over the world? I felt helpless. Gregory asked me to look at the world differently from that point on. He asked me to shift the angle of my kaleidoscope lens and begin to see new shapes.

I had already been clearing my inner lens through spiritual awakening, but I now looked at the outside world through a changed lens. I started to notice something that I had not been aware of before. What surprised me was that I saw immense suffering on all sides. The visible and invisible ashes had fallen on everyone. The perpetrators, the victims, bystanders and many innocent people are all linked up in a cycle of violence. We are individuals, but not entirely separate from one another.

Gregory said to me, **"We are essentially One."** He explained that one person's actions and words affect other people. If a person throws a ball in a room, other people will feel the energy regardless of whether the ball hits anyone or not. On earth, we see separation and differences. Our egos judge by appearances and discriminate according to our own narrow values and belief systems. We put labels on others and ourselves, mainly who is good and who is bad, or who is "one of us" and who is not. Gregory said,

"In truth, we are part of everything in this Universe. We are all interconnected, because in God there is no separation.

What you do to others, the harm or the good, you do to yourself. The consequences of your words and actions will one day come back to you. The hate you send out to others will one day be returned at a later time and through another experience. If you hurt someone, later someone else would hurt you. Your world is so tough because you have made it so tough. The misguided beliefs, wrong actions and mind games infiltrate all parts of your lives."

I understand what Gregory was saying. We think that there are good guys and bad guys. We want to believe that we are the good guys and the others, however narrowly we categorize them, are the bad ones. We set up rules and games to fight the bad guys in order to preserve our own goodness. But who are the bad guys? We can be both the good and the bad guys, depending on our thoughts and actions. The dark and light is not only outside of us, but also within us. The evil actions of some individuals cannot be generalized to any groups of innocent people, be they religious or political groups. These kinds of misguided perceptions and beliefs are great sources of violence and conflict in our lives, as well as in the world. In truth, each of us has a soul and is unique; we are all responsible to make this world a more peaceful place.

Gregory showed me how the world needs more compassion. If we are essentially "One," then we have to shift our consciousness to this truth. And love is the best tool to heal the sickness in this world. Gregory explained,

"There are solutions that can bring healing and peace, but the process of peace in your world is a long way off. But it can be done, when each of you takes the responsibility to bring healing and peace. Every positive action can overcome the negatives. I say that love and peace begin at home."

Yes, in the state of this troubled world, love and peace have to begin at home. How can we create peace at home? What is love and peace? What are the right things to do? To assure ourselves that we are doing the right things for our children, we often do what everybody else is doing. We walk the narrow conventional path of pressuring our children to succeed academically and financially. We push and micro-manage them every moment of the day to ensure their future success. We schedule their activities back to back: sports, music lessons, tutoring or whatever we think they need to succeed. After all, as we see it, their success in the world is ultimately ours.

After September 11th another and broader vision is emerging with my strong desire to raise the consciousness of peace and love in the world where my son and his generation live. I am committed to do my drop-in-the-bucket share. Life is more than about succeeding or failing in this competitive world; it is about including others through kindness and compassion.

When the pressure for our children to succeed is so great and is pursued at any cost, so much gets missed along the way. Hugs, encouragement and fun are also part of childhood. Too often, our children feel pressured to travel the fast lane to adulthood. Nonetheless, most of us parents struggle to do all the right things that we've been taught. I know this struggle well, because my parents, who were both teachers in Hong Kong, were not fluent in American language and culture, but well educated in the Chinese language. They read Chinese stories and told us of Chinese history. Unfortunately, at the time, this had little value in the competitive American classroom. So, we children had to struggle on our own in the American educational system; our parents couldn't help us; they had their own struggles in a new country.

Overall, the American cookie-cutter style of parenting, which is conventionally doing what everybody else is doing, does not guarantee parenting success. Where do we parents go for advice in difficult situations, when a child may need something particular from us? On a grander scale, what should we be communicating to them to help them bring more peace and love into this troubled world? Are we missing something? Gregory said,

"Your world is a schoolroom. The family is the first classroom for your children. They learn what you communicate about love, values, beliefs and behaviors. For example, if your words say one thing, 'I love you' and your actions do the opposite, your children get mixed messages. What the student learns in the first classroom, at home and with his family, he passes on to other classrooms: school, community and the rest of the world. The world is the biggest classroom that contains all other classrooms. The strife in the world is a reflection of the tension and struggles in smaller classrooms, with many lessons to learn and many more not yet learned."

If the family is the first classroom for learning love and peace, what must we parents do?

Gregory asked me if I would write a book with his help. Surprised, I asked on what? He answered that it would be on another way of engaging in family relationships. I replied that he had the wrong person.

Who would listen to me? He laughed, **"Why not you? You have been working on this book since the day you were born. Look at the rich materials from your life experiences and your search for answers."**

Divine Spirits have helped me to reconnect myself to my own heart. I recall my sad and confused childhood and my search for deeper understanding of human nature. My mother's pain has passed on from one generation to another in the traditional Chinese culture. In my work I saw the array of psychological problems that parents and youths have in their relationships. I also feel the immeasurable suffering among the families who had lost their loved ones on September 11th and in the wars that have followed.

I had been pondering many questions. What is conditional love that has too many requirements and unconditional love that does not? How can we change a cultural or emotional legacy so that we don't burden the next generation? Is there something special inside each of us that can guide us? To truly reach our children, we need to connect more with our own hearts. Then, with a healing heart, we can better connect with our children, heart to heart. My own heart has been silent too long.

With great doubt, I could not imagine what I, as one person, could do to affect the world. Gregory heard my skepticism.

80

"You are one person, but we are One Spirit. The September 11th event is undeniably painful with lasting impact on everyone, particularly on families who have lost their loved ones. They live with the loss every day. Also, for many groups of people who are not involved with this tragic event, they may live in fear of discrimination. I say this must stop. The old mentality of us against them or the division between the good and bad guys doesn't work. Hate against hate only brings more hate."

"You need to change the way you think about yourself and others. You need to understand who you truly are: *spirit on an earthly journey.* Your spirit is eternal. You can reframe the way you treat one another and your misguided beliefs that have been taught to you. You must begin to understand yourself and your world from the 'center of your heart,' not from your ego. The heart is the source of all love and wisdom. It has an expansive consciousness of it own. Love is the answer and the heart is the greatest healer."

I asked Gregory what kind of book we'd write. He replied,

"It would be whatever you choose. This is not a book in which I would dictate materials to you and tell the readers what to do. This book is a collaborative one, in which you experience the process of your search for answers and I am pointing the way for you. Think outside of the box."

For a long time, I stubbornly resisted working on this book. It seemed like a massive task. I was like the Biblical Jonah in the Old Testament. Jonah sat in the belly of the whale for three days, refusing the do what God had asked him to do. He eventually relented. I, too, resisted my task, avoiding writing by filling my time with distractions and making excuses. However, to my surprise, Gregory filled my consciousness with many ideas so often that I had to stop what I was doing and take notes. Annoyed, I would say to Gregory, "All right, all right. I will write down your notes!" These notes built this book as if it had already been written!

Mahatma Gandhi has a famous saying: "In the eye of the Universe, whatever you do is ultimately insignificant, but it is very important that you do it." I had no idea what to write. I did not have the bigger picture, but I was willing to thread the smaller pieces together like the patterns on a quilt.

I worried about readers accepting Gregory's credibility. His voice was alive to me, and I wanted to make it alive to the readers. I could not always make a clear distinction between where his voice ended and mine began. However, I have separated his voice from mine to give emphasis to his distinct wisdom and energy of love, as well as to his unique personality. Gregory told me that he did not care whether others believe he is real or not. He said, **"The message of love and wisdom is what I want to get across. Even a work of fiction holds truth. Let the readers take whatever truth this book holds into their hearts and let the seeds grow from within."**

I remembered a Buddha story. In Buddha's days, his disciples pleaded with him to politically intervene, because invaders were killing his people. Buddha sadly looked away. He said that it was not his work to stop the mass violence because change must come from each person. Thus, it is up to each of us to decide to act on the change. I remember another quote by Mahatma Gandhi: "Be the agent of change that you desire." Each of us is the change itself: we are the peace and we are the love.

The world is at a shifting point: we will move either to greater awareness of our humanity or to greater chaos. How the shift happens depends on each of us. The situation challenges us to become more aware of who we truly are. Each person is the center of change. The first change must come from inside, in our heart and mind, then with our families and eventually branching out to bigger groups. Each of us holds the power of good and evil.

Now, the first step for me was to make personal changes by taking a closer look at my own shadows: the sources of my anger. One source was the traditional Chinese belief in male favoritism. The other source was the painful and conflicting experiences between my dream for a more socially just world and the harsh realities in this world.

7. CULTURAL SHADOW BETWEEN MOTHERS AND DAUGHTERS

~

A traditional Chinese belief has inculcated a long-standing historical tension between Chinese mothers and daughters. To value sons more highly as the cornerstone of social prestige and honor is to displace daughters to a lower social standing. Over time Chinese mothers have passed this legacy down to their daughters, as if such a belief were the central tenet with which to define family relationships. For a daughter, the strain of this muted tension marks the journey from childhood to motherhood. For daughters, silence is golden and unquestioned duty is honorable.

When I, the daughter, became a mother, memories of my childhood brought emotions of both love and anger to the surface. I did not want male favoritism to dictate what I ought to do as a parent. I wanted to be the loving mother that I had desired. However, the past cast shadows on my parenting. Sometimes, bits of anger snuck up on me while I was unaware.

My mother passed her cultural/emotional history on to me. Standing on the cliff of the twenty-first century, I am still making sense of her history in relation to me. What do I accept and what can I change? I am speaking for many Chinese daughters who also might be struggling to understand their mothers. Male favoritism has cast a long shadow over the emotional relationship between mothers and their daughters. It has a significant psychological impact on the meaning of being daughters. For women, successive generations of difficult and painful childhoods layer the complex emotional legacy. A mother who felt worthless as a daughter likely passes on the same sentiments to her daughters, who would likely do the same to their daughters.

Being a parent is a complex role where many points of the past, present and future converge. Mothers have their past and are in the present with their children, but it is the children who hold the future. Such complexity has no easy answers, as the questions are often unspoken.

As social worker, parent, and spirit, I search for answers to the wordless questions. Perhaps, the emotional rift between mothers and daughters may be the same one that creates a schism within one's self. Perhaps, the lack of maternal love extends to lack of self-love. I seek to understand what is the love that touches me, and not just on the surface. For example, my mother and I had genuine love between us, but we could not communicate it, as if the old cultural beliefs stood as an emotional wall between us. In the Chinese culture, daughters are often caregivers for their aging parents. Yet, after decades of being devalued as daughters, this caregiving can be done as a duty, even with underlying resentment. Can caregiving be done with genuine love that touches the heart and breaks down the wall of misunderstanding? Can we daughters not pass this legacy on to the next generation?

Being a parent is not just about taking good care of your children's health and growth, although that is important. Neither is it about just getting them into college, nor about abandoning them on the roadside to fend for themselves in the name of teaching independence. Living with them every day for almost twenty years, we transmit our subconscious emotions and thoughts to them. We transmit our emotional history to them. Through their intuitive openness, our children absorb our unspoken language, the language of what love is or is not. We impact their lives by our example and action. What we don't understand, they won't, and they'll have to ask questions to find their answers. What we share intimately with them, good and bad, they take into the future. To some extent, the children we have been, our children become. Our history is theirs, too.

I have traveled this path. Life is like a pilgrimage. I imagine myself a pilgrim on the Camino de Santiago in the ancient Pyrenees, walking hills and valleys and passing villages and towns in search of insights. I want illumination on my path. A pilgrim doesn't just walk the road; she experiences the totality of the journey with all her senses, emotions, sight, changing thoughts and observations. She sees the dark and the light. Walking, she becomes still within and listens to the wind.

A Cultural Shadow

There is an ancient Chinese saying: "A picture is worth a thousand words." One time my father gave my aunt, my mother's younger sister, pictures of her village in China where she and my mother grew up. In the background stood an old house built over a century ago. This two-story cement house is now abandoned, with broken windows. Once upon a time, it was the village's meeting house. It had many rooms where children played when it was not in use. My aunt described how her mother (my maternal grandmother) took her grandson there to play with other children. Seeing this tangible building in her village, I saw fragments of my mother's childhood.

The Chinese mother-daughter relationship is complex. I am not just a mother, but also a daughter of a mother who had her own mother. The pride in having sons and the pity in having daughters are long-held beliefs. For example, women would brag about their sons to each other, supporting each other's good fortune, while they could say little good about the daughters. I have seen too many pictures of proud Chinese mothers with their arms around their sons, with the daughters left standing at a distance.

Growing up, I too stood at a distance in the midst of a family, feeling disconnected and looking into empty space. On some occasions, when I was angry, I also felt my mother's anger and her mother's anger, all reverberating down the ancestral hall.

The ancient Confucian philosophy has held traditional Chinese society together for thousands of years through its wisdom about family loyalty and duties. The practice of filial piety, respect for elders and unquestioned obedience are all parts of the social structure that has kept functional peace not only within the family, but also for whole villages. Each family respects the head of the household, while each head of the household respects the elderly leaders in the village. The peace might be superficial, but is essential for governance. Furthermore, the families care for their respected elders; and when these elders die, their spirits watch over the families through ancestral worship.

Men in the family wield authority. Their words are the rules of law. How the men of a household rule depend on their personalities. Some men rule with bad temper and foolishness, while some rule with wisdom. At the same time, sons are next in line to move into positions of authority when the elderly men pass away.

Sons are venerated not only for continuing the family name, but also for placing their mothers in higher social positions. Mothers of sons have more social prestige than mothers of daughters. To have sons is the purpose of every Chinese mother. The strong mother-son dyad actually has served as the backbone of Chinese family society, rather than husband and wife. Not only does the family name get passed on, but also the loyalty and love between them bonds the firmest relationship, in comparison to husband-wife, husband-son, father-daughter and mother-daughter. Sons reverently and dearly love their mothers, while the father and son tend to be distant. The father-and-daughter relationship is traditionally distant. Finally, the love between the husband and wife, in which the marriage is traditionally paired through matchmaking, is not considered important to society, so long as the couple perform their duties to the family.

The relationships between mothers and daughters have had a long-standing emotional tension. Daughters are considered worthless, outsiders belonging to their future spouse's families. The main purpose of mothering daughters is to prepare them for their future marriage. The separation process for a girl begins at birth! The strict discipline and limited maternal love prepare the young girl for her harsh life ahead in marriage. The preparation included foot- binding, running the household, preparing food for festivals and performing duties for ancestors. Expression of maternal love is usually guarded and restrained. Criticism and strict discipline are the methods used to train daughters for their future role. What is overlooked is that this is a harsh childhood with little love. Parents do not want to waste valuable and limited resources on daughters who don't belong to the family. Girls are merely temporary boarders.

Mothers pass on attitudes, values and practices to daughters. It's as if mothers are not supposed to love their daughters or, if they do, must keep that love inside because there is so much social pressure among other women to conform. The frequent criticism and lack of maternal love lead daughters to believe that they are worthless. Over time, the quiet anger of denial grows within and is conveyed to the next generation.

In this tightly woven social structure that has served Chinese families for thousands of years, change is difficult and slow. Beliefs and practices are so interwoven that even historical social change can't alter them— war, revolution or immigration to another country. Immigration, for example, only serves to replant the same roots in new soil.

My Family History

During the past century, in my parents' generation, women's roles in China began to broaden. When men could not be the sole providers, due to economic hard times, women helped support their families. My parents' and their parents' generations lived through several upheavals in China. Poverty, war, revolution, political corruption and chaos ripped through their lives. They had to find different ways to make a living and to survive. Women on both sides of my parents' families adapted to those changing roles, but this did not necessarily change the old practice of favoring sons.

My father grew up in Guangzhou, Southern China. Once upon a time, several generations of his families lived in one large wealthy household. Many of his ancestors held prestigious positions as scholars, statesmen, teachers and merchants. It was not unusual for husbands to have many wives and children. Both his father and mother came from well-to-do families and were children of men with multiple wives. My paternal grandparents married through traditional matchmaking. Because my grandmother's family was wealthy, as part of the additional dowry, her family gave her a year's supply of clothing and food. In the event the marriage did not work, my grandmother could return to her own family without taking provisions from her husband's family.

An interesting anecdote reflects the changing times: my paternal grandmother's feet were only half bound. In the middle of foot binding, which reflected wealth and prestige, her family stopped it because it was no longer considered fashionable. Her feet were very small but not bound! My paternal grandmother faced great challenges during the wars. Her husband's family wealth got scattered as the multigenerational household broke up into smaller units. My grandfather had to work in a distant town, while my grandmother also worked to support her two children. She taught elementary school for many decades, because she was among the small population of women who had finished their high school education.

My father gave me a brief background of how she came into teaching. Her older brother, who was a secretary under General Sun Yat-sen, the 1912 revolutionary father of China, started a primary and high school in their childhood village. Under his direction as the principal, my grandmother ran the whole school, hiring teachers and also teaching herself. Funded by the government along with their own private wealth, they built an important educational institution free of charge to the village children and teens.

It seems that my paternal grandmother had to find her own answer to being a woman and mother in China. She became an independent woman with a teaching career and was a devout follower of Buddhism. As for her children, to obtain a better life and education for her daughter, my paternal grandmother sent her to a relative, who lived in Malaysia. Her son, my father, lived with her until he started high school. She allowed her children the independence to find their ways in the world.

While my father's families lived in the big city of Guangzhou, my mother's families lived farther away in a remote mountainous region called Toisan. Farming was the main livelihood. At the turn of the century, living off the hard land provided barely enough to feed a growing family. As a result, an increasing number of Chinese men began sailing to the "Mountain of Gold" in California. My maternal grandfather was one of them. Shortly after he got married and had a son, he sailed to America to find better wages. He was interrogated at Angel Island, an immigration post off the coast of San Francisco, and luckily passed his test. He eventually travelled to Boston where he had a brother in the laundry business. Ten years later, he returned to China for a few years, during which my mother and her sister were born. When his daughters were very young, he returned to Boston. Though he continued to financially support his family in China, he never made enough money to return. I met him once as a five year old, when I first came to America. He was so happy to see all his children and grandchildren, but he died the following spring.

During World War II, without the physical presence of her husband, my maternal grandmother single-handedly raised her children and grandchildren in China. Her son and his wife had six children, with the oldest grandchild close to my mother's age. With money sent from her husband in America, she frugally managed to feed her large family during the war. In times of food shortage, she had to pick and choose which ones to feed the better food and which food to feed the remaining ones. Usually the daughters and granddaughters got the leftovers. With so many responsibilities, my grandmother had little time and patience for her daughters. Furthermore, her bad temper kept a firm control over the large household. My grandmother gave her devotion to her son and his family.

When my mother was young, she was close to her paternal grandmother. This grandmother (my great-grandmother) lived off and on with many of her sons' families, who were close by in local villages. Being a quiet and gentle person, her grandmother did not rule the household like the traditional mother-in-law of sons. She herself was said to have had a very hard life. Before her marriage, she attempted suicide by drowning, but was rescued. It's not clear to me why she attempted suicide—to avoid marriage is my guess. She later married an abusive and opium-addicted husband with whom she had nine children: five sons and four daughters.

The lives of my ancestral grandmothers were very hard. Each found her own way of coping, for better and worse. Women sometimes committed suicide as a way to the end suffering. However, some defiant young women, who vowed never to marry, lived in groups and sustained their livelihood through weaving and farming. But most women persevered through the suffering the best way they knew and adapted to the changing times. What they left behind are the emotions from their suffering: anger, low self-worth, depression and deprivation of maternal love. The tension between mother and daughter often reflects those emotions.

I feel deeply for my mother. Out of her hardship and sadness growing up in a household with little warmth and limited food, she learned that there wasn't enough love or food. The golden bits of love and food went to the precious few males, while the girls got the leftovers. With her own children, even though we had plenty of food, my mother seemed to perpetuate this belief in rationing love from an almost empty cupboard, as if the war were still going on. The physical war was long over, but it had become a war within herself. She had to give so much as a mother of three and had so little love in reserve for herself. This led to her lifelong depression.

My mother reminds me of a yellow rose (her favorite flower) that never quite bloomed. She did not have strength to nurture her tender roots, but nonetheless she stood firm and courageous. She was always kind to others, but not to herself. Her lack of self-love was reflected in her relationship with me. We bridged much of that rift when I became a mother, and we learned to understand each other better.

In my teens and early adult years, I made up my mind not to continue the cultural legacy of male favoritism and devaluation of women. Through my higher education and through examination of my beliefs, I was determined to treat all children equally. However, I overlooked emotions that I still had that lay heavy in my heart.

Like continuous silent films, the cultural shadow still projects shades of darkness on relationships from one generation to the next. When a mother is too caught up in believing there is higher status in having sons, she overlooks her daughter's value and denies her feelings. The mother herself has been emotionally denied and invalidated, as her predecessors had been. Chinese women from one generation to another silently swallow their pain.

8. MY DREAM AND A NIGHTMARE

~

As a child, I dreamed of a lovely garden here on earth, a place similar to somewhere far away that I vaguely remembered. That dream was planted in my heart. Growing up in the hub of New York City, I saw life through the kaleidoscope of my sensory experiences. As a curious child, I embraced life on the lower East Side with openness and without judgment. (I was too young to judge experiences other than with childish likes and dislikes.)

In our first apartment, we lived next to a small synagogue. Every Friday evening and Saturday, we heard prayers, music and chants. Later we moved across the street from a Catholic Church, which many Puerto Ricans patronized. During feast days, we watched colorful processions going into and outside of the church. On our way to Chinatown, we passed Jewish matzo factories, where my siblings and I watched through the windows as the conveyor belts moved the crackers along. The aromatic smell was tantalizing. Sometimes, nice workers handed out matzo to us.

In Chinatown, we saw and smelled succulent roasted ducks, pigs and chickens hanging in the store windows. We loved the roasted pork buns our parents would buy us for a snack. Our parochial school and church in the heart of Chinatown served both the Chinese and Italian communities, because Little Italy bordered Chinatown. Half of our class was Chinese and the other half Italian. I don't recall any problems between these two groups of students through nine years of grade school. Occasionally, I went uptown with my father to Mount Sinai Hospital, where he worked and which bordered on East Harlem. Through the innocent eyes of a child, I saw New York City as a diverse biosphere of humanity co-existing amid a cacophony of sounds, sights and smells—a place of infinite possibilities.

Perhaps partly, because of that rich experience in my childhood, I dream of a better world: a place where people are compassionate and where human dignity, equality and respect prevail. This world is not a utopia; I hold onto the belief that human compassion can triumph over indignities and suffering. If we try hard enough, we can overcome any kind of barrier, and people can arrive at better understanding of one another.

My high school experience proved such a possibility. After grade school, my family moved from New York City to Boston. I attended a public high school in the greater Boston area, where the students came from all different racial and ethnic backgrounds. I do not recall any of the racial tension there that was so characteristic of Boston public schools during the '60s and '70s. Instead, in our high school in Boston, a group of us from diverse backgrounds formed a club called "The International Club" in which we met weekly to discuss the richness of each other's cultures. I enthusiastically embraced this diversity, believing that people could not only overcome intolerance, but also participate in many cultures.

When I married a wonderful man outside my own background, we saw no barriers in our differences, just richness in the diversity. My dream was to foster universal oneness, because I intuitively knew that we were somehow connected to something bigger than we could imagine. I lost sight of this dream for a while, when an unexpected nightmare occurred. After I got married, we lived in a community just south of Boston where my husband had just bought a house. I was among the few minorities living there. My sensitivity showed me that the majority regarded me as a foreign specimen, and this attitude was a shock to me.

To be closer to my new home, and after many years of positive professional experience in the Boston area, I worked three years in this south-of-Boston community, not knowing at first what I would encounter. Right from the start, I experienced hostility from associates who formed cliques along color lines; I was the only non-white person. Their message was that I was "not one of them." Prejudice doesn't need to appear as directly assaulting another person or tossing out racial slurs. It can also appear as a collection of little snippy remarks and underhanded attitudes that have the same effect as overt prejudice.

This harsh awakening broke down my dream of equality and human dignity. I was effective in my work with clients, who came from diverse backgrounds. I understood the human heart, and they responded to my outreach. However, I could not deal with the prejudice of my co-workers. I did not know how to fight back. Unfortunately, this problem of divisiveness only reflected the bigger political situation in the agency where I worked. For a period of time, the institution lacked a director. The competition for power and control among the co-workers was fierce. They collectively regarded me as the marginal person with no professional credibility. I knew that I could not win this battle. This experience, along with my doubts about the theoretical nature of psychotherapy, caused me to leave the social work profession. I was burned out, from fighting a war on two fronts.

In retrospect, I wonder what contribution I might have made if I had stayed in social work. Did I give up too easily? I had my full accreditation as a Licensed Independent Clinical Social Worker and knew I had professional abilities. But, at that time, I had a strong intuition brewing in my mind. I began thinking of the need to explore the nature of spirit in psychotherapy. I once innocently commented to one co-worker that the spiritual nature in psychotherapy might offer an unexplored frontier for treating patients. This social worker took my suggestive remark as an affront to her expertise in therapy, although I did not make such an implication. Gossip went around, and the whole group then shunned me. Looking back, I was just ahead of my time with this unconventional thinking. Today, spirituality in psychotherapy has gained increasing popularity as an alternative approach to treatment and for personal growth.

Sadly, after I stopped working and became a new mother, the experience of prejudice took an even more personal turn. Being a mother meant that I spent more time in the tight, homogeneous south of Boston community where we lived and where my white mother-in-law lived with what she called "her people." I felt as if I were Alice, in *Alice in Wonderland*, who fell down the rabbit hole, landing in a world of strange characters. These characters—like the White Rabbit, Dodo Bird, the Mad Hatter and the Queen of Hearts—were neither good nor bad, but odd and self-absorbed in their tiny worlds of illogic. They played out their absurdities with intense seriousness. Alice tried to fit in. Her physical size changed from scene to scene to adapt to the context of others' realities, which were always changing and grossly incomprehensible.

Down the rabbit hole I went, into the land of mothers in a community that was unfamiliar to me, as I was to them. Everywhere I went within that community, I wore my irremovable label, "I am not white." It didn't matter that I was well educated; I was the outsider. My many interactions with my mother-in-law and her people also ran along color lines. I suddenly represented all non-white people: Blacks, Hispanic, Asians and others. What I really represented was the face of fear.

A few sporadic incidents of intolerance from a few individuals would have been insignificant, but the accumulation of negative experiences spanning many years left me despairing. When I went shopping at stores, sometimes cashiers would be very rude; this is nothing new and could happen anywhere and to anyone; but this was different. One time, I brought cosmetics and the cashier refused to ring up my items because she thought that I got the wrong shade of cosmetic powder: too light. I almost left, but instead, I demanded that she ring up my purchase and said that my selection was none of her business. Sometimes I observed that white women customers would, at the first sight of me, grab their handbags and run away to the next aisle, as if I was going to steal their purses. Goodness, what harm could a mother with a cute baby do? Sometimes neighborhood mothers corrected my accent because mine was not like their proper Bostonian accent with their "da" and "ah," because I had grown up in New York City.

There were nice individuals in this community, who were unpretentious and down to earth. My husband said that he had given away his Yankee heritage to the Salvation Army long ago. My father-in-law's own parents came from Scotland for a better life; he was a humble man. Some kind-hearted mothers invited me over for coffee while our children played. Nevertheless, my anxiety became acute, because I never knew when the undignified and petty assaults would occur. As my sensitivity heightened, the outside world looked scary to me. In that community, I took shelter in my own home.

Fortunately, young children don't understand prejudice. Beginning when my son was three years old, he and his neighborhood playmates went to each other's houses. His friends loved coming over to our house to play. I welcomed them with nice treats and fun activities. I could easily reach their hearts, but not those of most of the adults. In retrospect, it seems strange that, despite the mothers' snippy attitudes toward me, they trusted their children with me.

For example, when my son was in kindergarten, he had a playmate who lived three houses over. This playmate had been spending a lot of time lately playing at my house. I had heard that his mother was sick. One particular day, he was extra hyper, talking and running faster than usual. I asked him what was going on in his life. He looked anxiously at me and said, "My mother is going in for surgery today, and I am not supposed to know this. Of course, I know." I asked him how he felt. He answered, "I am scared and worried about my mother." I acknowledged his feelings. That day, I fixed a nice lunch for the boys and let them happily play all afternoon.

Prejudice and intolerance are learned behaviors, not part of an inborn human trait. Based on theories of child development, if toddlers are put into one room, they will play without judging any differences between them. They may see visual differences, but will attach no prejudice to their perception. However, less than two decades later, they will acquire enough attitudes from the adults and the social environment to exhibit much prejudice, little prejudice, or none, depending on what they have learned.

Many years later, two of my mother-in-law's former friends, who had recently passed away, spoke in my dreams. One woman said that while living on earth in her comfortable south of Boston community, she was "blind as a bat;" that she saw only through hindsight. Another person, a man said to me in another dream that he had not realized how small his community was in comparison to the universe. This is my interpretation of these two dreams; they were not so much apologies as they were expressions of broader understanding from the Other Side. An unquestioned value system and the mindset of a community can play a significant role in influencing people's behaviors toward others, especially those who look different. Their behaviors derive out of ignorance and social pride, rather than malice. At the same time, these few individuals could not represent the general sentiment and mindset of all community members. I am sure that many people don't feel or think that way.

When my family escaped to a more diverse part of the country in California and my son was in first grade, I climbed out of the rabbit hole to breathe fresh air again. This new place just outside of San Francisco had its own problems with competitiveness, but I had a fighting edge to maneuver my way through them because I was part of the many cultures there. The children in the schools were like the United Nations in their diversity.

Upon my return to Massachusetts in 2003 after thirteen years in California, we moved to a suburb twenty miles west of Boston, where we now enjoy living. Whenever I go back to that community south of Boston, I notice how much the demographics there have changed, because more minorities are moving in. I, as one person, could not change the community's jaded attitudes, but another generation will speak its own voice in the slow process of social change.

Recently, a young woman with whom my son played as a child in that south of Boston neighborhood spoke in my dream. She gave me her name and said that she had been looking for me to thank me for the fun times she had at my house. She said that she was sorry for the neighbors' attitude toward me. I told her to move forward and share her love with everyone she meets on this planet. This is the only way to reduce divisiveness. Maybe it was just a dream, but I was glad that I might have touched one person's heart and, through her, helped keep alive the hope of a better world.

I wonder if my son, when he was a preschooler, noticed what I was going through living in that community. We have never openly discussed that period of time, but he clearly observed much. He grew up experiencing the two cultures: the white American culture, of which is he a part, and the Chinese American culture. He appreciates both sides. In recent years, I have observed that he makes sure he expresses respect for all people and all cultures around the world. He values friends and colleagues for their strengths in character, rather than for any other criterion. Respect for everyone is what I wish for him and many in his generation, as a way to break many barriers and see the common good in all people.

I haven't given up my dream for a more peaceful world. However, this dream has shifted to wishing that more people would recognize their divine spirit and heal the barriers of separation and prejudice. I wish to see a reduction in people's tendency to fight for superiority, power and control at the expense of others. These endless battles leave no victors, because we all stand to win or lose together. As human beings, we are bound by One Universal Ocean, in which one wave affects all other waves. We as spirits have lots in common beyond physical appearances. We are not a mere shell of our egos. Inside our hearts, we all desire the same things: happiness, joy, peace, love and harmony for our children and ourselves. However, just listening to the news or reading the newspapers, violence and hatred are still everywhere. My heart tells me that we are a long way from such a dream.

9. A WISER HEART

~

Having experienced many good and bad dreams in my life, I had arrived at a critical point in my quest: I knew love was the answer, but my childhood love only taught me unworthiness. The feeling of low self-worth that was tainted with much anger sometimes spoke loudly to my dear son. When he asked if I would still love him if he were bad, I was shocked. What did I say and how did I say those words? My little child-teacher woke me up, driving a compelling determination to change my legacy.

Love on earth is mostly conditional, conditioned by family and by the value and belief systems in our society. How is conditional love different from unconditional love? I have experienced both, feeling the contrasts and similarities. Love has many variations and varying power, like the different brightness in light bulbs. I have learned that conditional love casts shadows of fear; it causes unworthiness and anger. On the other hand, unconditional love brightens the entire room and creates glowing self-confidence. I want my child to feel worthy of my love without any doubts, and that love is what I wish for myself.

Through understanding the differences between these two kinds of love, I have become wiser.

Effects of Conditional Love

I remember an observation that showed how conditional love is intricately woven into our everyday communication. I was at an animal clinic where I'd taken my sick cat. In the waiting room, a mother, her five-year-old son and their dog were also waiting. The little boy got off his mother's lap and wandered into an examination room. She called him back, saying, "You are being a bad boy going in there." He returned to her lap and sucked his thumb. A little later, he again slipped off and wandered into another empty examination room. His mother grabbed him. Annoyed, she said, "You are being very, very bad!" She pulled him back onto her lap. He quietly went back to sucking his thumb.

I thought that this little boy was just bored and curious, not being bad. Another response might have been to tell him not to go into those rooms for safety reasons and explain what they were used for. While this incident is minor, the mother's words suggested that the boy was a bad kid, and if such words are used too often, this labeling might lower his self-esteem. As busy parents we forget the subtle ways conditional love is written into the words we use.

In cultures, values and belief systems shape relationships. Although different cultures may have different belief systems, the effects may be the same. Both my mother's culture and my mother-in-law's culture seem to send the same message that there are certain requirements for lovability. In the Chinese culture, I was not a son. I could not raise my mother's social status. In my mother-in-law's culture, I did not have white skin. Having white skin, and especially being a white person of *Mayflower* descent, means privilege and power.

My Spirit Guide, Gregory, shows me that both kinds of value reflect "social pride" which runs along the same continuum. Such pride forms the conditions for a love that is selective and therefore divides people: the haves and have-nots. This division creates imbalance. For those precious few individuals who meet the conditions, what does pride really do for them, except perhaps to give the temporary satisfaction of possessing self-importance? Does it help them to be stronger people in the face of adversities in life? Does it help them to be compassionate? Not necessarily. What happens to those who don't meet the conditions? They may face lifelong struggles with self-esteem, self-love, unworthiness and anger. And they may perpetuate these feelings with others in order to work out their own pain.

I recall an unusual encounter many years ago that shed light on the effects of conditional love. I attended a recruitment lecture by a psychiatrist for a new approach to psychotherapy. Afterward, I shared with the group that my father-in-law, just before his death, had streamed his energies to me while I was talking with him. This psychiatrist said that it was common for a dying person to stream energies to others and that I had the sensitivity to pick up this streaming energy. His perceptive comment revealed something new: energies have power.

Then the psychiatrist then said to me, unbidden, "Your energies are all warped, as if you have been twisted into many knots. There are people in your life who don't value you and have put you down." Surprised by his insight, I asked myself how could he know? In an audience of fifteen people, we were all strangers to each other. This was the first time I saw myself as a composite of warped energies! When someone devalues you, he sends negative energy that warps your energy system, little by little. I didn't know that conditional love could twist a person's energy.

Love is powerful energy! We send love's energy out to others through our everyday speech and actions. We often are unaware of the subtle ways that we convey our love to others, because we live by habits, with little thought of the impact we have.

When I was growing up, my mother used sharp words scolding me.

I often felt frightened by her voice, as if every little mishap pointed a finger at my personal failure. Unfortunately, on the unconscious level, I took on her habit of yelling and scolding when I became a mother. I frightened my young son by the tone of my voice, because I didn't really understand that I sounded so harsh. My son was my teacher when it came to changing this habit. In retrospect, I wonder if my grandmother frightened my mother with harsh scolding too.

Conditional love gave me little happiness. I tried to please the disapproving others to get their affection, but my actions brought me no closer to their liking me. Then I came to an important point of awakening: my own heart is the center of unconditional love and peace for myself. I need not go outside to find it; it had been right there inside me all the time.

The Power of Unconditional Love

Several earthly teachers of unconditional love have enriched my life. My son and my husband have opened their hearts to me. They are nonjudgmental and accepting of me. They may not understand what I am going through, but they always love me.

Strangely, another teacher of unconditional love was my German shorthaired pointer dog, Melly that lived to a grand old age. She was exceedingly hyperactive and dumb. Her high physical energy level outpaced her intelligence by far. When I was young, not having had any pets, I was afraid of dogs. Warming up to her was difficult for me, but she eventually won my heart. Dumb as she was in learning tricks, Melly had her charm: she loved everyone. One day I heard an inner voice telling me that this dog was in my life to teach me unconditional love, and she did. I learned patience and appreciation for her. She gave us lots of laughter when she did dumb things. Not only did she teach me unconditional love but also "unconditional happiness!" Imagine being happy without conditions in this world! She was a very happy dog. Today, I smile when I fondly think of Melly and her funny ways. Our pets are often teachers of unconditional love.

Gregory, my special teacher and spirit guide, is my greatest teacher of unconditional love, simply because he knows me inside and out. He sees me clearly. His love for me is pure and powerful, with no conditions, no barriers, no judgment and no pretenses. I smile when I think of his joyfulness. I wanted to know the difference between conditional love and unconditional love, as if they were separate entities. But Gregory explains that they are not separate. Conditional love and unconditional love are at opposite ends of the same continuum. Conditional love is tainted with fear, while unconditional love is pure. The more positive and pure love is, the more powerful one becomes. On the other hand, the more conditional the love that one experiences, the more constricted one feels.

Gregory clarifies, **"All love is real but not all love heals."** He explains that love won by meeting conditions feels real enough, because the receiver of this kind of love feels good for a while. The receiver may get affection and/or rewards. But this kind of love is weak in that this energy of love only goes so far and then runs out, like a depleted battery. When the affection wanes and the conditions change, the receiver may be denied of love. In other words, conditional love sends mixed messages and gives in limited measure.

In the Cinderella fairy tale, the wicked stepmother conditionally loved only her two biological daughters but not her stepdaughter. She lavished on her two girls lots of material goods with the hope of one of them would marry the prince. She had beautiful dresses made for them for the prince's ball, while she deprived Cinderella of any hope to attend. But, in the end, Cinderella won the hand of the prince. The love that the stepmother gave was in half measure: limited and partial. Her hope was not realized. Had she loved Cinderella as one of her daughters, she would have had one of her three daughters marry the prince.

Once we broaden the definition of love to include more people, we can feel its expansiveness. Unconditional love is expansive. Gregory explains,

> "Unconditional love heals and transforms because it's a fine electromagnetic energy that exists on a higher and wider spectrum. As of today, it cannot be scientifically measured, but it definitely can be felt and experienced. It contains powerful vibrations that radiate their effects everywhere. A spark can light a fire. Your spirit is made of this pure and finer love energy. There is a powerhouse already inside each person; only most people don't know this or use it."

Gregory means that conditional love can be felt as love, but it doesn't last long. On the other hand, unconditional love is powerful and transformative; it's eternal. For example, a couple may love one another as long as each meets the conditions of love. When conditions in the contract of love are not met, their relationship dissolves and sometimes turns into bitterness. However, with unconditional love, even when the marriage is over, this love can be transformed into a platonic friendship in which each can continue in some ways to support the other. Unconditional love forgives, but conditional love does not.

Another story illustrates the power of unconditional love. *Silas Marner* by George Eliot is one of my favorite books. The main character, Silas, loved to hoard money. Wrongly accused of theft, he moved to a remote village, where he lived in isolation. His work as a weaver brought him a modest income that he frugally saved. Every night, with happy obsession, he counted his increasing wealth. One day, a passerby saw the money and stole it. Silas was devastated. As the story unfolded, someone mysteriously left a baby girl by his door. Silas named her Eppie and raised her as his own daughter. Her innocent love changed him forever. Their love took him out of seclusion and enabled him to discover the gold that was hidden in his heart. This story is about love's transformative power.

Gregory's unconditional love has transformed me. He shows me the gold that is already in my heart that I have forgotten; I already have so much love. He never judges me. He knows too well that I have already pronounced severe judgment on myself. Over almost two decades, he has patiently clarified my misguided thinking and negative emotions. He does so with gentle empathy and compassion. He understands that, living on earth, one can easily absorb the gross negativity around, which blinds one to understanding what pure love is. He asks me to value myself when others don't and tells me that self-love is the first step to loving others. He reminds me that I live in a society in which people don't always treat each other fairly and with respect, that their behavior doesn't reflect who I truly am.

Gregory explains that I can't change others to see things my way; rather, I can change my reactions to them. He points out that I expect a lot from myself and likewise from others. However, people often have very different standards and values. My dream of brotherhood and peace is mine, not necessarily another person's dream. Each person responds to me according to what he knows and how he feels about himself as well as me. Therefore, an unkind attitude toward me says more about the other person, as long as I refrain from provocation. Sometimes, I have to just walk away and let the other person be.

Gregory encourages me to be my true self. He says,

"Spirit is who you truly are. Spirit has infinite potential and expansive ability to love. On earth, the ego, which people see as the real self, is but a small fraction of who you are, at best, if it is not distorted. Think of yourself as a magnificent star in the universe. Your ego looks like a tiny cluster of molecules in a big star. Yet, you hang your identity on that one tiny nail, as if that is all there is. What you don't realize is the enormity of your true self."

Yes, I am working hard to be my spiritual true self and act from the center of my heart. I still have all my problems, but I am managing them better. With wiser choices and actions, I have more harmony in my life.

In the meantime, Gregory reveals to me something about my mother who is now in Heaven. He says, **"She loves you but she has lots of problems of her own. Forgive her. She has changed, but you won't know of this change from where you are. We do."** As for my mother-in-law and her community, Gregory tells me, **"Regardless of their attitude toward your ethnicity, your family—you, your husband and son—has set an example of love that shines like a beacon of light that transcends barriers."**

Unconditional love is Light. I ask Gregory for the courage to let go and be at peace with myself. I thank him for teaching me about unconditional love. He answers, **"In Heaven there are no conditions for love. Love just is, pure, effervescent and eternal. Listen to the wisdom in your heart."**

Listening To My Heart

I am highly intuitive and can hear my heart speaking gentle wisdom. Yet I frequently ask myself, "Have I made this up? Who is speaking to me? What does this intuition mean? Is it guidance or wishful thinking?"

As I gain more skill and confidence, I slowly recognize that my heart has a mind of its own: a tender voice of love and guidance.

I remember an incident that taught me about intuition. One afternoon, when I was about to head out for the half-hour drive through the narrow canyon to pick up my son at school, I heard my inner voice telling me to wait fifteen minutes. Fifteen minutes late would mean a delay in my pick-up, but I followed my intuition, leaving a bit later. As I drove, at the beginning of this narrow canyon road, I saw that an accident had just occurred. A passerby was holding an injured man. The next day, I read in the local paper the injured man had died. I was shook up. Would I have been involved in that accident had I not listened to my intuition?

To trust my intuition, I must pay attention to the whispers of feelings in my heart. My intuition may say: "Have you thought of this?" "Try that approach." "Try again." "This person doesn't see things your way; back off." Then I examine the truthfulness of the intuition and ask myself whether or not it is relevant.

How can I believe in something that is not tangible and not validated by my physical senses? Our physical body has five senses: smell, touch, sight, hearing and taste. But intuition is the sixth sense that many have forgotten to use, because its awareness is not considered real. Intuition is connected to an inner awareness that comes in whispers of words, a feeling, a piece of information, a premonition or a flash of vision. People can easily dismiss an intuition for being illogical or as wishful thinking.

There are several ways to differentiate wishful thinking from an intuition. One is that an intuition never forces a person to do something against his free will. One always has the choice to follow it or not. Secondly, it never tells one to harm others or oneself. Third, it is generally an inner knowing of a higher good for others as well as oneself. It may come as a warning not to do something, or an insight about someone, but it never takes away one's freedom to choose.

I envision my heart as a communication center, in which I hear not only intuition but also voices of Divine Spirits. I cannot always figure out if an intuition is from my self, my Higher Self or from Divine Spirits, but that doesn't matter. It is still from the same Divine Source: God who may even be talking directly to me. Through meditation and a growing recognition of my intuition as a powerful source of love and guidance, more and more I rely on this communication center.

Intuition also teaches me to trust my choices and to make better decisions. I may ask my intuition questions and surprisingly get answers. Should I do this or that? My intuition helps me see that I have choices and how each one can bring different outcomes. Making better choices brings better outcomes.

For example, I do not believe in the Chinese legacy of male favoritism. What do I want to change for myself? The lack of self-love is the part that I want to change. Lack of self-love comes from the self-denial that Chinese mothers have taught to their daughters. Chinese culture teaches that mothers, as caregivers, are supposed to put their families ahead of their own needs. The culture demands self-sacrifice. This self-denial leads to feelings of unworthiness and compromised self-esteem.

Gradually, my intuition has taught me self-love. With my family of origin, being a daughter and a middle child, my only recognition comes from being a caregiver. However, as I grow in spirit, I see myself as worthy of respect and love. I am not just a mother's helper. Self-love has been a very hard lesson for me to learn. How do I learn to love myself unconditionally when I have not experienced unconditional love? It is also very difficult for me because caregiving is part of my personality. I am learning the balance between caring for others and caring for myself. My intuition has helped me to make better choices in attaining this balance: when to give and when to step back and reserve love for myself.

I also use my intuition to guide me to improve parent-child

communication. I learn to listen actively with my heart to what my son is saying, without judgment. In doing so, I refrain from too-quick reactions and overreactions and become more thoughtful with my words. By being more in tune with what he is communicating, I am able to give better feedback and more helpful advice.

Moreover, my intuition is also teaching me about the components of unconditional love. In all parts of my life, I practice empathy and compassion, because this unconditional love enables me to see that all of life is interconnected in oneness. What one person does to another, she does to herself. To me, empathy is emotional identification with another person's suffering. We can't take on others' suffering as our own, but having empathy helps us to understand it. The love we feel for another person connects our heart to hers, and empathy helps us to put ourselves in another person's shoes. Compassion is empathy in practice. It creates a path that renders kind actions toward, and caring for, one another. When we feel another's suffering, we can act to help alleviate that suffering. If we cannot alleviate another's suffering, we can simply be helpful to others in ways that our intuition directs us.

Without empathy and compassion, the misdeeds we do to others, or others do to us, are often done out of ignorance. This ignorance often derives from lack of awareness rather than from malice. People who are angry or depressed say and do thoughtless and hurtful things without being aware of how they affect others. If they were more aware, they would be more careful of their words and actions. Furthermore, I have observed that we are often disconnected from our own hearts when we thoughtlessly hurt another person. We don't feel their pain because our own pain has overwhelmed us. Listening to our intuition is an important way to connect to our own hearts, as well as to be compassionate with others.

My Mother's Final Journey

A huge life lesson faced me with the question, "What could love do?" As my mother approached eighty years old, her health was failing. A series of strokes had rendered her increasingly disabled and helpless. I put aside my anger over her conditional love for me. I put aside old resentments and bypassed my childhood memories of her criticism. She became a person, separated from being my mother, one whose lifetime of accumulated struggles had led to her current state of immense suffering. I wanted to be compassionate and reach out to her. I couldn't make her well again, but I could give her my pure love. My heart was my inner compass to guide my actions.

Her illness opened her heart, too. She let go of her worries and expressed her love to all of us. Now her heart and mine were open. I did everything for her from my heart: cooking nourishing foods, bathing her and helping others to take care of her. I sprinkled in extra warmth and kindness. We even laughed a lot; she called me her "rescuing angel." The love I was giving her was also the same love I wished to give to myself. Through my actions, the joy of love was seeping into my heart.

After my mother's second stroke, I witnessed a miracle. Over a weekend while she was recovering in rehab, my mother developed *petite mal* seizures, which eventually came on about every fifteen minutes. At dinnertime, I worried that she might choke on her food, should a seizure happen while she was swallowing. I talked to the nurse, who called the doctor for seizure medication. (My mother had not taken any before.) While waiting for the medication, I asked my mother if she would let me pray for her. She nodded. She, my husband and I held hands. I prayed for her healing. In my heart I quietly said another prayer: that she would return to Heaven of her own her free will, not from choking on her food. At that instant, her seizures suddenly stopped and never returned. She took seizure medication just for a few days. She lived another year with other difficulties, but without any seizures. I was glad that I had listened to my intuition and appreciated my husband's collaboration in praying for her.

When I look back on my life with my mother, I know that, behind her harsh words, her love for me shone through in many things she did for me. She made me clothing and brought presents home from her many travels with my father. Most importantly, she listened to me as a loyal friend when I needed sympathy, and she was my great shopping companion. I miss her but her spirit is still with me.

My father, of whom I have spoken little, has survived my mother. He is living well into his nineties. In the process of my taking care of him, we have grown closer and have had opportunities to talk about many subjects related to family, culture and even metaphysics. He does not believe in male favoritism, but he grew up in that same kind of male authoritarian environment, so the attitude still comes through sometimes. Nonetheless, I love him dearly.

I am not implying that unconditional love will always bring such immediate miracles. In fact, most of the time it does not. Rather, it provides the course for natural healing and subtle transformation to occur over time. Unconditional love is always guided by the wisdom of one's heart—and I mean always, because it brings unity and healing even in a most difficult situation. By making choices that resonate with your heart's intuition and taking the higher road in your words and actions, you give unconditional love the power to work miracles. The outcomes are greater joyfulness, peace, harmony and goodness.

Through the many lessons I have learned about unconditional love, I have now completed part of an inner journey. The search for deeper understanding has bought me to an important personal transformation point; I am looking at life, and particularly my life, through a clearer and more loving lens. I am now a little wiser in my heart. In the Bible, 1 Corinthians 14 says:

"For now we see in a mirror dimly, but then face to face. Now I know in part; then I shall understand fully, even as I have been fully understood. So faith, hope love abide...but the greatest of these is love." 1 Cor. 14:12–13[4]

10. HEART-CENTERED PARENTING

~

My son has inspired me to be a heart-centered parent. I recall an incident when he was in the seventh grade. At three o'clock in the afternoon, I waited in the school's parking lot, which had already emptied out. I saw my son slowly walking toward the car. He got into the car and angrily slammed the door. He said that he'd had a bad day. As I listened, I wanted to give him my conventional wisdom about what to do. I even wanted to intervene by talking to his teachers. As parents, we like to give lots of advice and are very protective. However, the inner voice in my heart told me to say nothing, but just to listen. My heart became a mirror reflecting what he was really saying to me. I toned down my rational and fix-it-all attitude and shared with him what I heard him saying. With empathy, I reflected his frustrations. By the end of the trip home, we were happily chatting about other things. Thereafter, he was better able to handle problems himself.

This incident was a defining moment for me. Instead of reacting to his frustration, I listened to him and also to my intuition. To get to that moment, I had done years of work on listening to my own heart and believing in myself. Parent and child are reflective mirrors of one another, deeply connected or deeply disconnected.

Unconditional love is the only kind of connecting love that works, and one that our children know. Fresh from Heaven, they are the embodiment of Light/Love. (Light and Love are the same things: a unit. One cannot speak of one without the other; they are simply pure and powerful energies.) Parents of a newborn actually gravitate toward their baby's Light/Love, which has a translucent radiance. As children grow, they show surprising loyalty and affection. Their ability to love and accept their parents reflects their unconditional love. When I worked with abusive families, the abused children had unwavering loyalty to their parents. These sad children believed that their parents would get better and love them again.

If children's love is unconditional, then, to reach them, parents' love has to be unconditional too. The limited give-and-take of conditional love, given in bits and pieces, leaves little in the bucket of love—and material goods cannot fill it. If we fill their hearts with our unconditional love, we leave them with an unlimited amount of love to empower their future. How do we reach them? Heart-centered parenting simply means to let our hearts guide us and to love them unconditionally. We give from our hearts to theirs, as theirs are given to us. They trust us to love them.

Over the years, I have learned and observed a lot about parenting. Its most basic foundation is the heart. Indeed, it is only with our heart that we can see clearly. There we know what our children need from us and what we should do for them. Our heart is our inner compass to help us navigate the parenting of each child. Someday, by keeping his heart open, the child will use his own inner compass to guide his life. If we close our heart to our children, they will close their heart to themselves.

The Heart Is A Service Center For Parenting

In the Chinese language, a community center is called "*jun-sum*," which literally translates "middle heart." In any given community, residents go to this center for many services: health care, meals, legal consultation and so forth. Within a family, children go to parents for care services. Our heart is the center that has the true ability to organize parenting matters and help us to act thoughtfully. Most of us parents are already working from our heart center. We dearly love our children and do everything we can for them. However, we sometimes follow conventional wisdom to guide our actions; we act in accordance with social rules and what we have learned from our childhood experiences. With little questioning, we perform our role as we have been taught.

Parents wear many hats: teacher, coach, judge, nurse, chef and playmate. We make sure that our children are safe, nurtured, provided for and guided. Sometimes we are asked to make split-second decisions and sometimes to come up with long-term strategies. At times, our patience runs thin and our temper snaps. We parents cannot see the contradictions between our thoughts and our actions. Without awareness, we rely on the habitual ways of doing things that may not always work. For example, if a child seriously misbehaves, it is necessary to punish him and withhold privileges to teach him. However, how we are feeling and thinking about everything else at the moment affects how we discipline. If we are angry, we will yell and make reactive decisions. The reasons for the misbehavior vary in each situation and for each child. The questions to ask is: What is the cause of the problem, and what is the best way to teach the child not to do it again? The place to handle those particular challenges is in our heart: the community center from which our services should proceed.

Parents of special-needs children know well the daily challenges. Michele Pierce Burns is the mother of an autistic and gifted child, Danson Mandela Wambua. Danson is unable to speak, but through the use of a machine called "Facilitated Communication," he is able to express his thoughts and feelings cogently. He speaks of his intense frustration as well as his love for God. Through painstaking and persistent effort, Burns wrote down her son's articulate poems, which form the book *Danson*. He expresses his anger at not "being able to speak" and observes that "...we only lean on God more when we are scared."[5]

Parents like Michele Burns have to listen and follow their hearts. Parenting takes them on uncharted roads, full of uncertainties and compromised expectations. Unconditional love in the center of our hearts is the central agency to assist us when we travel such roads.

Parents without special-needs children also find themselves wondering what are the right steps to take. When that happens, we need to ask if our assessment and understanding of the problem is clear or if our own personal emotions and biases are clouding our perceptions.

For example, when my son was then fifteen years old, we watched a documentary about juvenile delinquency. Probation officers described how impossible and mindless delinquents were. My son laughed and made an astute comment, "Those officers sounded like they had never been teenagers before." How true. They forgot what their own adolescence was like and how impossible they were then. Adults sometimes act as if teenagers are of a different species. Empathy seems to be difficult for them.

Another example of the disconcerting experience is the psychological tension between Chinese daughters and their mothers. When the daughters become mothers to their own daughters, they may echo sentiments of the past about male favoritism. In doing so, they perpetuate the legacy of double standards for sons and daughters. These Chinese mothers may not realize that they have choices: to pass on this destructive legacy or to change the course. A mother's heart will tell her that she has a choice. This is a very important point in changing any legacy that one does not want to repeat, be it a cultural value, emotional/physical abuse, or any painful situation. If and when he listens, his heart tells what those choices are. Each one of us has this power to change. As for myself, I have tried to make that choice with my son, not to exhibit the attitude of valuing boys more than girls.

The Heart Has an Inner Compass

Heart-centered parenting provides an "inner compass," like a GPS that guides one on a journey. Since children do not come into this world with manuals, how to guide them is sometimes a guessing game. If this inner compass were to speak, it would ask parents, "What would love do?" This question helps me when I am making decisions. If I examine my thoughts and feelings, the voice of my heart differs from the voice in my mind. In other words, my "thinking mind" offers a different solution from my "thinking heart." When I am angry or worried, I don't listen to my heart. Rather I let my run-on thinking rationalize: my son should do this or should do that. The words "should" and "must" suggest pre-judgment, a block to clear understanding.

When I worried about my son, I perceived the negative, what he was not doing right, in my opinion. I would criticize him and he would react defensively. However, if I listened closely to my heart, I could see that he was doing many right things. Instead of being quick to criticize, I backed off and quietly observed. My heart would perhaps tell me to try a new approach, or to do nothing.

The heart has clarity of its own, different from the conditioned and reactive mind—although we must use both our minds and hearts together in many situations. When I was doing therapy with families, I worked from the voice of my heart to understand their problems. On one hand, I relied on my clinical training to do assessment and treatment; on the other, I learned to tune into my heart for guidance. One time, I worked with a group of graduate interns who were working on clinical hours. I noticed how much they relied on academic learning to do their work and overlooked the important process of introspection and self-awareness. A therapist himself is the change agent, rather than his therapeutic methods alone.

In addition, the heart holds our thoughts and actions in balance. In the "middle heart" center of parenting, we stand at the fulcrum of a seesaw. The word "seesaw" connotes keeping a balance, so we don't want to go into extremes. Dan Millman, author of *The Laws of Spirit*[6], writes that this balance is important. If we overdo or underdo something, the pendulum will swing to the far right and then to the far left, throwing us off balance. Balance allows us to focus on what is important and on not doing too much or too little. We need to walk the middle path.

If we push our children too far in order to fulfill our own dreams, they can fail or rebel. Or if we don't care enough to hold them to higher standards of behavior, they can be lost. To keep a balance means to know the right thing to say and to do the right thing at the right time. We cannot expect to be perfect, but can correct the imbalance through listening and following our hearts in our care for our children. The heart knows when to try harder with our children and when to let go, with the latter being more difficult. On that afternoon during pick-up time at the middle school, when my son was upset, it was best to let go of my advice mentality and to simply listen.

Furthermore, our hearts can tune into emotional cues. The sixth sense helps the parent to pick up nonverbal gestures, like facial expressions, and the feelings behind unspoken words. For example, a parent using his heart can perceive subtle facial gestures and other body language that the child is showing, although not saying anything. Through observing emotional cues, the parent can obtain more information, such as that the child is scared and frustrated rather than just being mean. Without tuning into emotional cues, it is so easy to miss subtle gestures that give insight.

In today's busy world, each day we are constantly multitasking, living off our to-do list from moment to moment. We parents overfill the calendar with activities and are obsessed with our smartphones as they assist our multitasking. We think that we know exactly where we should be and what to do. As we check things off the list, time moves us through the day, on to evening and to bedtime rituals. Then another day begins with the same procedure. This intense busyness makes parenting all that much harder.

Life is hectic, for sure. However, the heart center is the best place from which to parent. It fills us with patience, kindness, creativity, balance, playfulness, joy, intuition and most importantly, unconditional love.

11. INTO YOUR CHILD'S HEART

~

Heart-centered parenting refers to connecting our own hearts to our children's hearts. There we hear each other and truly connect with love. Through love, we feel how special we all are to one another.

Every child comes to earth in a unique package, with her own personality, mission and lessons to learn. The inner compass is in the heart. When we use our own inner compass, we activate our children's. When we are connected heart to heart with them, they will then listen to us. Then, someday, they will listen to their own heart.

I have learned many lessons about how to get into a child's heart. One involves better communication. How can we say what we mean and mean what we say consistently? How can we better listen to children and get them to really pay attention to what we're saying? What are some effective tools for communication?

Another lesson is that the foundation of a person's character is built in the heart. If we want our children to possess good values and to develop strong character, we must reach their hearts. They don't develop character through our endless lectures of "I told you so." Rather, they learn through our heartfelt connection with them. They need us not only as role models, but also as gentle coaches. Strong character is built from our hearts to their hearts.

And one more very important lesson is the value of praying for our children. Praying comes from the heart, declaring our love and concern, regardless of what religion one belongs to—or even if one has no religion at all. I pray for my child. Not only that, when my son was in high school, we came together as a family to pray.

Effective Communication

Words and actions are major tools of communication. I recall a common childhood chant: "Sticks and stones may break my bones, but words will never hurt me." In truth, words hurt as much as actions. Abrasive words, over time, deeply bruise a person's psyche as much as hitting a person with a stick wounds the body. The intention is the same: to hurt. The effect verbal abuse has is hard to diagnose in the victim, because it bears no physical scars, whereas physical abuse is easy to see. Thus, words matter at least as much as actions, because their effect is buried in the psyche.

Furthermore, unspoken gestures, tones of voice and innuendo are very much part of communication. You can say much without spoken words and you can hint at hostility indirectly, without confronting the real issue. The other person can observe and feel the message from this kind of unspoken communication. Hostile tones, darting eyes or contorted facial expressions say a lot. Indirect and snippy comments are other ways to express hostility.

As a parent, I go by the motto: "Say what you mean and mean what you say, but don't say it mean." There are three parts to this motto: "say what you mean," "mean what you say," and "don't say it mean." These three parts, in order to be effective, must go together. They are like three horses pulling a wagon—they need to go the same direction.

If I say one thing, then do something contradictory, and do or say it in a mean way, the effect is lost. If I wish to go north, but my words go south and my actions go east, I won't arrive at my destination. For example, if I want to teach good eating habits, I forbid my child to eat cookies before dinner. Then I eat cookies before dinner, myself, thinking that he is not watching. The next day, I bake more cookies. Then I use cookies as rewards/punishment, saying that he can only have two cookies if he behaves well. What is the message? My child would battle with these questions: Is it right to eat or not to eat cookies before dinner? How am I supposed to behave? What are the rules? Why can Mom eat cookies without rules? Why don't Mom's actions and words match?

We affect our children in subliminal ways through nonverbal actions and gestures, which our children have to interpret. We had a very smart gray and black striped cat named Tiger, who was my son's special kitty. Tiger was the second of two cats and knew how to dominate an older black female. When he was just a kitten, he figured a way to attack the bigger cat. He would walk backward toward the black cat and then suddenly turn to attack her. A fight would ensue, and I would yell at Tiger. I then would pick him up and put him in the closet for a while to calm the situation. Over time, Tiger continued his attacks but afterward walked himself into the closet. He learned the procedure by heart, and I needed no words or actions. I said what I meant and meant what I said consistently. I probably acted mean, too. In retrospect, I wonder what else I could have said and done differently because I felt bad for Tiger, the self-punishing cat.

In my social work caseload, I worked with a seven-year-old boy who had behavioral problems at home and in school. He told me that his parents often said that he was a bad boy. In his young mind, a bad boy must misbehave all the time. The communication was clear to him as to what he should do.

Effective and consistent communication poses challenges in finding the right words, right gestures and right actions that go together. We have been wired and conditioned to say and do certain things in certain ways. We may even think this is an expression of love. We are not aware of those old destructive habits and how they affect other people. Yelling at my six year old for not picking up his toys to the extent that it scared him scared me too. I then questioned not only "what" did I say but also "how" did I say it, all those emotional tones that I was not aware of.

To children, our words are like the promises that we make. We can keep promises or break them. When a child is two years old, we use promises to distract him. "If you behave, I will buy you a toy." We know that we won't get to the toy store for many more days and hope that the whole incident will be forgotten. But if we make promises to a five year old, he will remember the promises and, over time, hold them in his heart. In my professional work with troubled families, I saw too many divorced parents making promises to show up for custody visits but never showing up. I remember seeing the painful faces of their children.

Even if we parents can't see our contradictions and hypocrisy, our children do! Not only do they watch us, they also act out what they have observed. After a while, they know how to push our buttons: through the gaps in our communication.

The heart is the center from which to map out our words and actions. The wisdom of the heart has unity, with its ability to think,

145

feel and speak cogently and act cohesively. Our heart will take us to the right next step, so that we can find the right words and take the most appropriate actions. Furthermore, heart-centered communication enables parents to feel and reflect more deeply, so that words, feelings and actions will express a common goal.

Here are four guidelines for improving communication:

Be aware of our thoughts and feelings. In order for me to say what I mean, I reflect on my range of emotions in the moment before my words dart out. What do I really want to say? I can be in a good or bad mood, unrelated to my child or his situation. My shifting moods affect my tone, choice of words, unspoken gestures and actions.

In an earlier chapter on the cultural shadow between Chinese mothers and daughters, I spoke of how the pain can be felt at all times. Because of her past, a mother can transfer her own resentment and pain to her daughter. Without awareness, a mother can easily say things that express her past anger or disappointment to her daughter. She can be harsh with her words and actions, as her own mother and her mother's mother had been.

Taking a few minutes of introspection on a daily basis to examine our feelings can make a tremendous difference. Quieting down, we can find the right feelings and words to say what we mean to our children.

We can pull ourselves together, instead of flying off the handle under stress. Our anger, for instance, can never justify our actions, because the anger is our own. We may feel disappointed and frustrated with them, and can say so. But hurling verbal abuse, shouting and hitting, in my opinion, are not the right ways of disciplining or teaching. When we locate our moods in our heart, we can hear our wisdom speaking kinder words to us—"Calm down." "What is the central issue?" "What is the truth?" There is another way that works! If I can't hear my own heart speaking, I count to ten or a hundred to create a pause before speaking and acting.

Listen with our heart. Besides listening "to" my heart, I also learned to listen to my child "with" my heart. What is he really saying and not saying? How is she feeling? What might he be thinking that he can't say? Empathy and compassion are central to listening with your heart. When I listen with my heart, I put aside my judgment and criticism.

To master this skill does not come easily. I have an old habit of jumping several leaps ahead of what the other person is saying, eventually realizing that I missed something important along the way. This old habit can easily get me into a mindset of who is right and who is wrong. If only we slow down and truly listen with our hearts to what the other person is saying, we can piece together information with clearer understanding. For example, if a child has been sent to the principal's office for misbehavior and her parent is called in, the parent's immediate response is often embarrassment, anger and fear. The parent may reprimand and punish the child without truly listening to the other side of the story. Maybe a classmate is bullying her. In anger and in a hurry, the parent may not probe into the reasons for her misbehavior. When a parent does listen with the heart, it's easier to assess and handle a situation. After all, a bad behavior does not mean a bad child.

Make thoughtful choices. A common response of parents is blaming our child for our overreaction or choice of a bad response. A parent might say that her child "has driven" her to do this or that, but in truth that there are always choices, even if the choice is not to do anything. In the midst of confusion or a need for quick response, we react without thinking through the choices. But we have free will, and sometimes the fundamental choice may come down to a choice of attitude. We may like our child, dislike him or regard him as a bad or perfect child. If we shift such one-sided attitudes, changing the way we judge our children, we will see different choices. Sometimes, without thinking, we give such labels to our children. If we change the labels, or don't label them at all, maybe our attitude will change.

When we choose our attitude thoughtfully, we can see more choices. With thoughtful choices, we can make calmer decisions that will promote positive and healing relationships. Instead of regarding a particular child as slow and difficult, for example, we can see that he has some learning disabilities in which the normal standard has changed. Instead of seeing him as an embarrassment, lowering our self-esteem, we can choose courage and the willingness to struggle and work with him to do better.

Take responsible actions. Here, we do what we mean clearly and consistently. If we say that we will do A, we follow through on our words and choice. If we can't do A, then we determine an alternative choice and follow through with it.

Even when we make a thoughtful choice, we can still make mistakes in actions and consequently learn only from hindsight. Making mistakes is human; as humans we can be honest and correct them. The wrong thing about making a mistake is blaming it on others or on a situation. Somewhere in the course of any mistake, there should be a small element where we own and contribute to it. Thus, we can be honest with ourselves and accept responsibility to change that small part that we are responsible for.

For instance, a preschool child doesn't understand the concept of time. In the small world of a classroom, she understands that she has to wait in sequence to be picked up. She thinks, "Mommy comes right after Johnny and Jamie get picked up and before Sarah's dad comes." One day, all her classmates' parents come first and she is the last one left. Her mother is stuck in traffic, running late. The little girl cries out of fear that her mommy won't come. For the mother to blame heavy traffic makes no sense to a three year old, so expressing how anxious she feels when she is late to pick up her daughter is a better choice.

More often than not, it is wise to apologize to our children in an honest and heartfelt way, not for every little misstep, but on important issues. I have observed that children are very accepting and forgiving. Apologizing is a sign of strength rather than weakness to them.

Communication through words, actions and gestures is an integral part of any relationship, because we are always in communication with our children. The energy of love keeps our connection constant. How we do so can make a tremendous difference: moving toward harmony within a family, or toward confusion and misunderstanding. If we think back to our childhoods, we can remember things that our parents said and could have said that would have made a difference in helping us feel good about ourselves. Our children need this kind of thoughtfulness in communication.

Building Character

Parents think that discipline, through rewards and punishment, is the only way to teach our children to behave properly. We believe that discipline shapes character, but in truth it is only one component.

When my son was school age, my husband and I posted a chart of rewards for completing chores on the refrigerator. When he did his chores, we applied shiny stickers. This tactic worked only for a few weeks, because eventually we got careless about stickers and rewards. Soon enough, the chart fell into the trash. We also tried giving him choices of A and B, but he would negotiate with us for his plan C. Strangely, his plan C made sense, too. More often than not, we would give in to it. My husband and I concluded that we must have marshmallows in our heads.

Fortunately, our son was a very good child with a mind of his own. To build good character and instill values, we reached out to his heart to show him how to make good choices and to be strong.

Why is building character an important part of parenting? The character of a person can be strong or weak, and it can sustain or break a person in hard times. Inner strength comes from the angel inside that shines the beam on the path. We live in a difficult world, where we have to learn to manage our own frustrations and anger. In times of despair we are called to be courageous. We are asked to be honest in the face of betrayal and lying. Life asks many things of us: to face the most difficult situations as well as ourselves with greater wisdom and greater compassion.

In building a child's character, saying positive words is important. My Spirit Guide, Gregory, reminds me, **"An ounce of encouragement is worth far more than a pound of criticism."** Let us affirm the positives rather than hammer our children down with negatives. Positive words of encouragement build up the foundation of character, while negative ones tear it down.

The Chinese language and the English language both recognize the importance of the word "heart." To describe a person, a word that precedes "heart" can reveal the character of the person. In the English language, "good heart" means kindness; in the Chinese language, the same combination of words mean the exactly same. A black-hearted person in English and Chinese also means the same thing, describing a dark-minded person, as the words "cold heart" mean someone without feelings.

However, some compound words in Chinese have different meanings from English. In Chinese, "poison heart" means evil; "little heart" means to be careful in Chinese, but in English it means to be stingy. "Big heart" in Chinese means careless but in English it means generous. "Hot heart" in Chinese means faithful, while in English it means "passionate." Whatever the combinations are, both the Chinese and English languages recognize the importance of the heart in expressing the character of a person. It is in the heart that we parents can teach our children strong and positive character.

In teaching patience, we should be patient with our children. In teaching compassion, we show them our compassion. In teaching honesty, we are honest with them. In teaching social justice, we are fair with others. In teaching perseverance, we persevere through our trials. And in teaching them self-confidence, we show them we believe in our own self worth. While we are role-modeling these characteristics, we also use encouraging words to build our children up in these areas.

Of course, we should say encouraging words only if they are truthful. Their expression has to be genuine. However, children are sometimes naughty, and their misbehaviors need to be corrected. Therefore, thoughtful, constructive criticism is necessary in shaping character. It is not only *what* we say but also *how* we say it that makes a difference. Harsh words and accusations are like pounding cement on the ground. Softer and firm words are like feathers. Instead of accusatory phrases such as, "I told you so" or "You are being bad," we can say, "I cannot accept the way you are acting. Let's talk about it."

My Spirit Guide, Gregory, is right. Any bits of featherweight encouragement outweigh pounds of criticism. Feathers lift and fly, while cement stays in the ground, going nowhere. As we build their characters, we also need to pray for guidance and for our children.

The Power Of Prayer

Prayers are important to my life. As I grow spiritually, sometimes unspoken words become prayers because my mere intention makes a statement to God. I remember an incident with my then 88-year-old father. I had called him in the morning and insisted that he not walk a mile to the center of town in the light snow that was falling. I worried that the snow would make the streets slippery. Being an independent and stubborn person, he went anyway. On the way home, he took the trolley back for only two stops. As he stepped down and backed away to let the trolley pass, he fell into a two-foot-deep hole that he had not seen and could not lift his legs high enough to get out. He called for help, but no one was nearby. Suddenly, two identical-looking teenage girls came to lift him out. He said he literally flew out of the hole. When he turned around, they had disappeared. He walked home safely. I think that they were angels. Divine Spirits were watching over him that morning.

In our moments of need, help is always available. I have had visions of angels everywhere, watching over us and always nearby to assist us when we call. Sometimes we don't even need to call them; they come anyway. There is an invisible energy that I call "Universal love" that comes to aid us when our souls call. Prayers express our "collective appeals" to Heaven for assistance or guidance. When we ask for help, we also must have deep faith to believe that our prayers will be answered.

A frequent question about praying is why doesn't God answer my prayer? My Spirit Guide, Gregory, explains that there are many reasons it seems this way, but for sure, all prayers are answered. First, we may not see the answer because we are fixated on a certain outcome. There is a story about a man who was about to drown in the flood. He called God for help. A boat arrived. He declined a boat ride by saying that he was waiting for God. A second and third boat came. He still refused to get in. Finally he drowned. In Heaven, he angrily asked God why he did not come to save him. God said, "I sent you three boats and you refused to get in."

Sometimes, the soul of the person for whom we are praying has a different destiny that we don't understand. Another person's will and destiny are his, not ours to change. Only the soul knows. A sick child may die despite prayers said for her. From the parents' viewpoint, their prayers have failed. This is not necessarily so, because the soul still benefits from the love energy of the prayers, which may be healing the soul and consoling the family.

Third, an answer to a prayer may come, but it comes at the right time or offers a better solution that works within the context of our earthly reality. An unemployed person may pray to win the lottery, but the chance of winning the lottery is rare. Instead, God may give him an opportunity for a job.

Through prayers we send good wishes and love to our family, friends and ourselves, and also to places in the world where it is needed. Through praying, we consciously organize the finer spectrum of unconditional love energy to help a person for whom we are praying. Perhaps this loving energy may assist the person in making more thoughtful decisions, in having clearer insights or in having the courage to take good actions.

I saw a bumper sticker that said: "Praying parents make a difference." We do. Our prayers reflect our deep love and care for our children. There are two kinds of praying—prayers for one's self, and prayers for others. When we know what we want, we pray for ourselves. However, prayers for others are a little different. They are called intercessory prayers. We intercede for these others. When praying for another person, we pray for the good we wish for him or her. The challenge is that we personally don't usually know of another person's soul destiny and her larger picture. In addition to asking for specifics to happen, we also must ask for the best outcome: this or something better, according to God's will. The next step is to be patient, have faith, do your best and leave the rest to God. Ask for, believe in, and wait for answers to come.

For me the hardest lesson in praying is learning to detach myself from the specific outcomes of my prayers. If God doesn't answer my prayers my way or immediately, I think He doesn't love me. However, what is important is not only *what* we pray for, but also *how* we pray. God knows us deeper and better than we do. Before we utter our first word in prayer, He knows what we desire and need. What God looks for is our feelings: heartfelt intention and the sincerity with which we pray.

When I first began to pray for my loved ones, I would ask God for specific things to happen or to be given, as if I was a child begging Santa Claus for specific toys. With little confidence in my prayers being heard, I implored again and again into the empty space. Sometimes my prayers were answered, but sometimes I didn't see the expected outcomes. Then I got angry. I remember an eye-opener. One evening, I screamed to myself that I could never win, implying that God was not answering my prayer! The next morning, while driving through the middle of town, a white car suddenly cut in front of me; I was mad. Then I saw the license plate that said, "GOD WINS."

Slowly I learned to pray differently with a fundamental change in attitude: I let God's will be done for the highest good, and I said thank you in advance. I also added, "This or something better according to Your Divine Will." Then I detached myself from specific outcomes. With this changed attitude and modified prayer, I saved myself much anxiety and trusted God.

Pray according to your religion or faith. Even if you don't have any religion, God listens to all prayers. God is above all religions, and with God all things are possible. Parents' prayers are almost always from places of unconditional love for their children: genuine and heartfelt.

When my son was in high school, we agreed to pray together as a family. Once a week, for ten minutes, we discussed our cares and worries and then prayed together. Over the next four years, we truly bonded heart to heart. Today, decades later, we still pray for one another, no matter where we are, in different houses or different cities. The power of prayer is infinite.

Humbly, I share what I have learned. These lessons weave into the heart of parenting. As guardians, we parents hold our children's hands as they begin their earth journey, and some day, soon enough, we have to let go. And from us they pass their lessons of love onto the next generation.

The heart is the center that we call home. We have this place in our heart to guide them, to love them and to provide fuel for their journey. When they grow up, they leave home with the love at their center, travel their own roads and return home again.

12. THE INNER CHILD

When my son was eight years old, he came home from school one day complaining of a tummy ache. I asked him if I could give him some medicine to make him feel better. He replied, "No, Mom, I want candy. Candy will make me feel better. I have to satisfy my inner child." Then, sheepishly looking at me from the corner of his eye, he remarked, "Mom, you know all about the inner child. Don't you?" I chuckled at how this young child could see through me. Impressed by his insight, I probably gave him a handful of candy!

Within each of us is an "inner child" who wants endless candy and goodies and who is also an angel. The youthful poet Mattie J. T. Stepanek eloquently wrote about his feelings in his poem "Night-Light Magic": "I am a little boy between an angel and a wild thing."[7] In the poem, he described his fears along with the joys of being an angel. He recognized that both are parts of his inner child.

Mattie Stepanek's poems displayed remarkable spiritual wisdom for someone so young. He wrote six volumes of poems, beginning at age three with the help of his mother, Jeni. His books included *Heartsongs*, *Journey Through Heartsongs*, and *Hope Through Heartsongs*. In 2004

Mattie died at the age of almost fourteen from his long struggle with a rare genetic muscular dystrophy. Over his short life in a wheelchair, he traversed more miles and possessed greater wisdom than many people who live much longer. He is remembered for his courage, intellect, and most of all, his passion for peace.

Mattie wrote of the inner child as the "cross between a wild thing and an angel." That is, the inner child is both an angel and the physical person. As an angel, the inner child is pure, unconditionally loving, open and intuitive. As a physical being, the child may be impulsive, self-centered and demanding. In this duality, each child expresses the magical contradiction of angelic exuberance and childish impulsiveness.

Parents need to tame the "wild thing" of the inner child, so that the child can adapt to a world of many compromises. A child can't do everything his way; he must learn to give and take in an imperfect world, as well as to develop good judgment. Yet, the child must keep open the "angel" so that it shines its Light in a world of darkness. The world is full of violence and fears, and a child's love can be an antidote to hate. The challenge of parenting is to know the difference between taming the unruly child and keeping open the innocence of an angel. First, let's look at the angel in each child.

Many years ago, I volunteered in the surgical ward at a children's hospital. I remember a special little boy in this unit. One time, the nurse wheeled him into the playroom and placed him on the rug. He had big round eyes and a bright smile. He rolled around and around with lots of energy, but he didn't have legs. His legs had been amputated due to a ravenous infection. He wore a skin-tight jacket to help his scars to heal. However, he seemed oblivious to his stubbed legs and inability to walk. As I rolled the ball to him, he squealed with delight when he caught it. His joy and enthusiasm equaled a winning player on a soccer field. This child was in his true angelic self.

What is the spirit of a child like? In his book, *The Secret Spiritual World of Children*,[8] Dr. Tobin Hart, author and child-development specialist, writes about children's spirituality. Dr. Hart identifies five unique spiritual characteristics in young children: 1) "Listening for Wisdom;" 2) "Wonder;" 3) "Between You and Me;" 4) "Wondering;" and 5) "Seeing the Invisible."

According to Dr. Hart, "Listening for wisdom" means that young children sometimes are able to grasp the truth faster and better than adults. For example, a child may say to her mother, "Watch out. That guy is not nice." Her mother looks surprised, because she is thinking the opposite about this person. The child can sometimes see through a person better and faster than her parent.

"Wonder" means that children are enchanted with their surroundings. The world is alive and present to them. They are always living in the "now" and have the ability to absorb the wonders of the moment, feeling of joy and excitement about life.

"Between you and me" means that children have an uncanny ability to empathize. This enables them to pick up others' feelings intuitively. While children can be self-centered in their thinking and sometimes act selfishly, Dr. Hart points out that they can also be unusually caring and generous.

"Wondering" refers to the curiosity and imagination of children. The backyard is a microscopic field for the study of nature. They ask many questions and wonder about mysteries in the universe. Sometimes adults hear children ask big questions about God. I remember at age six or seven, myself, asking, "What is the meaning of life? Why am I here?"

Finally, it is possible that children can "see the invisible." Through their sixth sense, young children are sensitive to the spiritual world. Many children talk to angels and deceased family members. They are open channels for divine communication. Some have invisible friends, whom adults call imaginary playmates, but, in fact, their invisible playmates may be real, even though adults can't see them.

Therefore, young children are more spiritual than we might think.

Along with being more spiritual, they have uncanny abilities to perceive, intuit and interact with the visible world and beyond. Their spiritual development is far beyond their biological development; they express their inner awareness through their illogical mind, which adults call imagination.

I remember an incident when my son was four years old. We were traveling in the region of Mesa Verde in Colorado. On the road, we stopped to admire the beautiful Painted Desert. Our young son quietly stooped down to gather little stones nearby. Seemingly immersed in his own world, he carefully placed the stones in a circle. Either he must have been closely observed the landscape, which had many circles of stones, or he was creating this circle from his own intuition about offering prayers on that sacred ground. My Spirit Guide, Gregory, points out,

"Children are indeed open channels; they can communicate with Heaven. They are highly intuitive and perceptive, even though their biological brains aren't matured in their reasoning. But their spiritual mind is clear and their heart is open. Children's spirits are alive! They listen to and follow their hearts."

Many adults have lost the ability to listen and follow their hearts as they walk through the illusions and delusions of the material world. Some adults go into therapy to reclaim this inner child. Why do we have to lose the inner child in the first place? What contributes to this loss, and what can we parents do to keep our child's inner spirit alive right from the start? The answer lies in keeping the heart's channel open through unconditional love and appreciation of our children's innate spirit.

Keeping The Heart's Channel Open

If a young child has an open channel to Heaven and joy is his natural state, how can we keep open this angel side through the growing years? It is through unconditional love, which opens our hearts to savor life. Each of us is spirit in a physical body on an Earth journey, rather than just a physical body with a big ego on Earth. From a child-developmental viewpoint, as the child physically matures, his spirit side generally quiets down. The reasoning ability of the brain overtakes intuition, which, according to society, is illogical and invalid. The logical mind and maturing body temper the angelic zeal as the child adapts to earthly realities. However, this tendency for the spirit to recede does not have to be absolute, because a child can stay spirited and loving throughout the growing years.

Dr. Thomas Armstrong, author of *The Radiant Child* and child-development specialist, points out that each child is essentially radiant; her soul possesses spiritual gifts and extraordinary love. The reason for each person to come to earth is to bring the angelic spirit into physical being; the soul knows its higher purpose. Dr. Armstrong uses the term "spirit down and body up" to suggest dual developments. "Spirit down" means that the angel side comes down into the body of an infant who will grow into adulthood. "Body up" refers to the maturation of the body and the brain. The goal of both spirit and body is to reach an integration through which the spirit, using the physical body, can express itself and fulfill its purpose.

On Earth, if life experiences are too negative and too painful, a person can lose her way. Very negative life experiences: abuse, deprivation and hatred can envelop a person in darkness and cause her to forget the inner angel, the diamond inside. My Spirit Guide, Gregory, tells me, **"Spirit soars or spirit hides, but spirit never dies."** Our soul is eternal, whether we express our spirit or not.

In other words, the soul comes to this world in a little spacesuit, which is the physical body. In this new little spacesuit, the soul at first remembers Heaven from where he comes. This is why young children are so spirited. As the spacesuit expands and grows, the person then begins to believe that this spacesuit is its only reality. The spacesuit eventually becomes his sole identity, dominated by the ego. Sadly, for many, the angelic inner child recedes over time. The angelic characteristics of intuition, pure love, enchantment, curiosity and openness gradually fade.

Love keeps the angelic channel open. The spirit of love is far more powerful than the physical body. It can overcome many obstacles. For example, I remember a story about a group of developmentally disabled children running a relay race. One child, who was way ahead, suddenly stopped running. She waited for all the other children in the group to catch up. The group spirit was far stronger in him than the spirit of competition. Through her example, everyone shared an experience of compassion and equality.

From my observations and life experiences, there is one particular way to keep the angelic channel open. That is to avoid labeling our children. Labeling pushes the angel side of the child away, because of the pain it causes. Labels are tainted with value judgment, prejudice and distortion. If a child has particular problems, such as learning disability, parents need to remember that the child is not the problem.

The Negative Consequences of Labeling

Recently I had a conversation with a dear friend. We come from very different backgrounds. She grew up in a white, middle-class environment on the West Coast and was part of a blended family with step-siblings through her father's remarriage, one very different from my family and culture. Over the years, we had held long discussions about our childhoods. But, one day, while we explored the topic of labeling, we were surprised that we both had the same family labels of being "overly sensitive and stupid." We discussed how damaging those labels were and how they were given within the context of the family dynamics. Both of us had struggled to redefine ourselves, but many decades later, those labels, which are hard to scrape off, still stuck to us.

I have worn many painful labels in my life. These labels reflected other people's opinions of me, but not who I truly was. I was not the embodiment of negative labels but had a brighter side that I could not shine outwardly. Not knowing better, I incorporated those labels into my identity. With Gregory's help it took decades to remove my labeling of myself and to let go of other people's negative opinions of me.

What are labels? We live in a world of duality and opposites. Labels come in superlatives of values—such as bad, good; tall, short; smart, dumb: stupid, clever; beautiful, ugly. Labels often compare one with others in lesser or greater terms. As children, we believe those labels to be real, because we don't know who we are and adults have to tell us. Later on, when we are parents, by habit, we do the same without thinking and label our children. The labels we give to our children oftentimes reflect the same labels given to us when we were children. This is how families pass on a legacy.

For example, as in traditional Chinese culture, a mother who was labeled as a worthless daughter, without thinking, passes on the same sentiment to her daughter. A father who struggled in school as a child may pass on the feeling of academic insecurity to his child. Labels are often projections, as if a faded film is still projecting dark shadows on the wall.

Let's look inside a label. As a child, I was labeled "too sensitive" because I sensed people's conflicting emotional messages through their words and actions. I got upset hearing angry words, whether they were directed at me or not. I believed that I was bad for being too sensitive, although, in truth, this sensitivity was my psychic gift of deep awareness. So, what was really a positive became a negative.

Besides labels, we may put our children into categories, which are similar to labels. Family, culture and society define the categories. For example, society categorizes a child as disabled, and her parents' worry reinforces this categorization. Parents, out of fear, may treat the disabled child in negative ways or see him as an embarrassment to their social status.

In addition to labels and categories, giving our children rigid family roles to play is also harmful. In many families, each child is assigned a role to play. Those roles provide equilibrium within an emotionally fragile environment; otherwise, the family would be in chaos. For example, some family members receive the roles of black sheep, clown, manipulator, servant, goody two-shoes or the baby. In abusive families that I worked with, certain children were picked to always be the troublemakers who deserved all the blame and abuse. Giving a role to each child serves to keep the dysfunctional family functional and stable, but the child loses the opportunities to grow personally. Thus, the suffering of each family member stays indescribably painful.

The traditional Chinese culture defines roles for children by gender and birth order. The oldest male, who is the head of the household, has the most power and prestige, and everyone else falls into respective positions. If there is unconditional love, there is nothing wrong with being called by a positional family name. Family members can still respect and love one another. However, if a title carries the connotation of power and control, then the roles of who is dominant and who is inferior can distort relationships. The dominant one may try to control the inferior ones, even though in true reality, no person is dominant or inferior.

The child who receives a certain label, category or fixed role has to figure out its meaning in his life. If he doesn't understand it, he will incorporate this role into his identity without insight. He will come to believe and identify with the given label, category and fixed role, which will become part of his ego identity.

I imagine the ego to be like a big cardboard box, rigid on the outside and dark inside. People stick lots of labels onto the outside of the box. Those labels can make the box fancier or uglier. But, inside, in the darkness, is a tender bud of spirit waiting to bloom. This bud needs sunshine and water to grow, not the darkness and the stuffiness inside a box covered with stickers. If a child never gets beyond the labels slapped onto the ego, his spirit won't have the chance to shine.

How can we get beyond the labeling process? One way is for us parents to see our children from a different and higher perspective: They are little angels from Heaven. We parents are their temporal guardians, but their spirits belong to God. We don't own them; they are precious gifts on loan. We love and guide them to young adulthood, but then we must let go. They have their own purposes for being here and their own missions to accomplish. With unconditional love, we will always be available for them, and they for us. Moreover, unconditional love possesses no categories, no labels, no fixed roles, while labels are the basic terms of conditional love.

Heart-centered parenting provides the tools to help us avoid labeling and categorizing our children. Following the voice of love and wisdom in our hearts, we can fine-tune the solutions to particular issues or problems and try different approaches to address problems. Our heart will guide us to say and do the right things. What we want as heart-centered parents is for our children to believe in themselves.

What a person believes she is, truthfully or not, she becomes. Mahatma Gandhi wrote:

> *Your beliefs becomes your thoughts,*
> *Your thoughts become your words,*
> *Your words become your actions,*
> *Your actions become your habits,*
> *Your habits becomes your values,*
> *Your values become your destiny.*

Beliefs, thoughts, words, actions, habits, values and destiny are all interconnected. Essentially, our beliefs eventually become our destiny.

We want our children to have faith in themselves. This faith will provide them with inner strength and direction in life. Our children will have unlimited potential and their personalities will be expansive, if they believe in themselves.

13. EVERY CHILD NEEDS TO BELIEVE IN HIS OR HER SELF

~

I knew a five-year-old boy whose parents and younger sister were athletic and played many kinds of sports. This little boy hated sports. His parents tried unsuccessfully to get him interested. He resisted by showing how incompetent he was in playing sports. Frustrated, his parents must have communicated their disappointment to him. He became disappointed with himself, often muttering to himself. Hearing his mutter, his parents began worrying that he might have mental health problems. To aggravate the situation, this sensitive young boy was kept back in kindergarten. He began to identify with his failures, losing faith in himself.

I, too, was a sensitive child who lost faith in myself. In my family of origin, I sought approval from my parents by being a good caregiver. I did not mind taking care of my younger brother or doing household chores to help my mother. However, my good behavior went unnoticed; but when I did something not to their liking, I immediately got yelled at.

As I grew older, I knew that my caring and nurturing nature was part of my inner angel. I had a natural compassion for people's suffering, with the heartfelt desire to help them. I also had an ability to perceive others' needs, especially to lift their spirits or to cheer them up. I simply could not be what I was not. Fortunately, my husband and son have valued my caregiving nature, so it does not go unnoticed any longer.

Growing up, and for a long time afterward, I believed that my caregiving was worthless, frivolous and insignificant. There are two ways to see caregiving. One is as giving with compassion from your heart; the other is as an obligation, in which you give with resentment.

When I asked my Spirit Guide, Gregory, about caregiving, he said, **"Who is your master? Who pays you for your caregiving?"** God is my Master and provides all I need.

Gregory explained more, **"Do you know that caregivers are healers when they give from their hearts? You are the healer and the healed."** What he meant was that as healers we give what we wish to heal in ourselves. We are in essence healing ourselves while we are healing others. We caregivers heal with our inner Light.

I think of the dedicated doctors, nurses, health-care professionals, teachers, workers who hand out food to the homeless, and countless other caregivers who help the sick, poor and needy. A child who starts a donation project for charity is a healer. All the ways we show our caring add up to making a difference in this harsh and divisive world. We need to understand that our caring and our compassion have impact. Gregory has shifted my ambivalence about my caregiving nature. That shift in my self-perception promotes faith in myself as a caregiving healer and understanding of my value.

Faith in oneself is fundamental to personal growth. I saw a video clip of a ten-year-old boy with ADHD. He and his parents struggled with this disability, as he was unable to control his impulses and to perform adequately in the classroom. By coincidence, he discovered his love for dancing, where his natural talent shines. Dancing requires both free and controlled movements that flow with the rhythms of music. His dancing has become the key to changing other aspects of himself, his approach to academic learning, and self-confidence. He now identifies with his passion for dancing and hopes to succeed in the world by working with that passion.

What a child identifies and expresses, he becomes. The strongest identifications are the emotional attachments, what and whom we love and fear the most. Our children can develop attachments to strong emotions—such as anger, fear, love and compassion. Another strong category of identification is whatever is most exciting and lucrative in the cultural environment. Children develop strong attachments to symbols in popular culture. For example, the subliminal influences of advertisements affect the psyches of young people. The seductive gestures of a sexy body, consumption of alcohol, driving fancy cars, or having certain electronic devices are enticing. These symbols might mislead our young people into thinking that doing and having those things could provide a fast passage from childhood to adulthood. This identification with the wrong emotional attachments and with popular culture symbols can camouflage the need for belief in oneself. By striving too hard for outward things, one forgets the inward dreams.

We parents are our children's guardians and the interpreters of what is right and good in this world. Through our relationship and our communication with them, we show them how to navigate the ways of the world, so that they can realize their dreams. Their dreams are part of their inner angels, which must be expressed. Yet, without parental guidance, our children will not know where and how to begin to reach for their dreams.

Abraham Maslow, a well-known psychologist (1908–1970), formulated the theory of self-actualization. To be self-actualizing, the individual must meet his hierarchy of needs before he concentrates on reaching positive potential. Besides the basics of food, clothing and shelter, this hierarchy of human needs includes physical and psychological safety, love and belonging to a family/community, and positive self-esteem. On some level, an individual must meet all these higher needs in order to realize and achieve full potential. We parents are here to provide for many of those needs, creating an environment for our children's growth.

We parents can learn how to create a safe and positive environment for our children. We organize their little world with wisdom in our hearts. We help them to develop good judgment and to identify with people and situations in their environment that promote their well-being. Each child has her own temperament, as well as dreams and goals in life, but life experiences also shape the personality, pointing to who a child will become.

I am sharing my ideas on creating a positive environment based on three developmental stages: infancy/preschool, school age, and adolescence. While children at an early age can express their personalities, temperament, and needs, they are still an open channel to new experiences and cognitive learning. Their personalities are not cut in stone, but are malleable and can be shaped. In each development stage, I suggest important tasks that our children need address, and what we can do to help them.

Infancy to Preschool Years: Feeling and Experiencing

Young children in this age group begin their lives with unconditional love and trust of their caregivers. From this perspective we parents also begin our relationships with them, giving them our unconditional love and building trust.

These children, who have no fixed ideas of their new world, simply "feel" and "experience" their daily lives. Their parents are the anchors for their experiences and feelings. Young children are open channels, with no specific identification with anything, yet. They have no judgment of what is good or bad; they simply experience interactions as being good and bad feelings; they also are learning to trust or distrust.

If unconditional love and trust are the foundation for our young children, how and what can we give to them? From my experience as a parent and a professional, I see several things. **One is to provide structure and consistency.** A baby learns of his new world through you. You interpret its meaning, and she loves you unconditionally. She counts on you to make her world safe, predictable and loving. Our most vital job is to give the young child safety, structure and lots of love. Love is the energy that feeds their growth, as important as food.

A baby needs to feel safe and not prone to injuries or hurt, both physical and psychological. She needs predictability from her caregivers, not only in behavior but also in affection and expression. She learns that when she cries, her parents respond; she needs to know that the responses are loving and consistent. When her caregivers make a promise to do something, she needs to know that she can count on it. Safety, structure, predictability and lots of love build the foundation of trust and good feelings.

Another is to recognize their spirited and intuitive ways. The magical years that are full of fantasies and natural actions are not merely a childish era to outgrow. They are the period of expressions of the inner child, which we as adults later try to reclaim. Adults may see magical thinking as being cute and fun, but it is a serious business for young children. Their magical thinking often reveals "the portal to their dreams and passions."

By this I mean that their imagination mirrors their dreams of future life work. A young child who fantasizes being a train conductor may not grow up to be one, but is learning skills and responsibility associated with this kind of role. A child pretending to be an actress may grow up to be a lawyer who later is able to act and argue in court. A child pretending to be a knight fighting dragons may be learning about being brave and honorable. Without judgment, parents can have fun just observing their children's fantasies, which provide insight into their inner dreams and passions.

Along with their fantasies, children's fears are strong. Some adults say that children have active imaginations. Yet, sometimes, those fears may have their roots from deep in a child's psyche. A child's strong fear may or may not be related to a safety issue or a trauma in the environment. An unrealistic and persistent fear is real to the child, even if it is not real to adults. Be cognizant of those fears, and help the children to work through them, instead of dismissing them as mere magical thinking.

Third is to enhance their empathy and kindness. Young children can easily flip between being selfish and being empathic to others: the child who wants and the child who cares and shares. When they act selfish or aggressive with others, it is not too early to teach empathy and kindness. Using puppets to role-play feelings is a wonderful tool. Parents can also role-model kindness to others. Most importantly, a parent's empathy for the young child is the key to his learning kindness.

School Age: Feeling, Experiencing, and Identifying

Feeling and experiencing all the different textures of life continues into school age years. Also at this stage, our children begin to strongly "identify" with significant others, role models, and important objects in their environment. When their thinking ability matures, children are now more aware of the bigger world. As their horizon expands beyond home, their exposure to the world broadens. During this period, they begin to identify with prominent features in their environment, at home and in society. They look for role models, ideals and heroes/heroines. They are attracted to certain character traits, such as kindness, compassion and love. They are also exposed to violence on television and elsewhere. They enjoy the challenges and entertainment of multimedia: Internet, computer games, smartphones and so forth. Their interest in, and possible addiction to, technological devices unfortunately has a mixture of positivity and negativity. Our role as parents is to be aware of how their activities help or hurt them.

For example, a documentary "Global Junk Food" (2016) points out the subliminal effects of advertising junk food in children's games. France has strict regulations regarding the necessity of posting nutritional values at fast food restaurants and guarding against direct junk food advisement to children. However, the fast food chains found ways to encourage eating junk foods by putting images of fast foods in children's video games. French parents have been alerted to monitor the games their children are playing on their computer screens.

Watch what they identify with. What are your children spending time doing? With whom are they spending time? Their activities and experiences will shape their thinking and emotions. For example, if one parent is particularly violent and erratic in behavior, without much love and guidance, the child can identify with this parent and become the same way. If a child identifies with responsibility and hard work, those traits can become part of him. If he enjoys sports, he will identify with them. If a child is labeled as being lazy and inattentive, those qualities can become part of his character. If a child has difficulty in school, teachers can identify him as a bad student.

Observing what children identify with will give parents ideas on how to direct or redirect their children's activities. For example, when my son was in middle school, he and his friends started playing computer games, some of which were appallingly violent. In my parenting mind, I wondered if I should stop him from playing those games. Was he going to identify with violence? I could set limits, such as allowing him to play games only when he was done with his homework or music practice. But he always did his homework and practiced his music, so that limit would have been ineffective. I listened to my heart, which told me that it would be all right for this particular young man to play those games. He was smart and discerning with good judgment. If I had forbidden him to play those games, we would have a power struggle, and he still could find another way to play them at his friends' houses. In retrospect, my son saw the violent games to be just games, and violence had no part of his reality.

Teach empathy and kindness and introduce problem-solving skills and cooperation. Empathy and compassion continue to be important to develop, as is teaching children that we are all interconnected. What one person does affects others. The good and the harm that we do to others affect us too. Increasing empathy and compassion brings forth awareness of this interconnectedness.

A Canadian classroom designed a project that taught empathy among school-age children. A mother came in with her baby once a week for students to observe the parent/child interactions and then discuss their observations. Over the weeks, the children learned to read the faces and emotions of the mother and baby. They developed empathy through learning to read the emotions of others. This Roots of Empathy (rootsofempathy.com) program has had a "significant effect in reducing levels of aggression among school-age children while raising social/emotional competence and increasing empathy." The model now has programs all over North America and Europe.

Bullying, whether in cyberspace or in person, is unacceptable; yet it is not always preventable. The perpetrator grossly lacks empathy and ability to feel others' pain. Perhaps sometime in his life he himself has been hurt or bullied. The perpetrator and victim lock themselves in the cycle of pain and anger that goes nowhere and solves no problems. A child who has been denied love will likely deny love to another, until the cycle is broken. Here is the situation where community members, parents, adults and peers can intervene to stop abuse in the moment, but the only way bullying will disappear is when all children are raised with love.

We as parents need to work together to make this world a better place. Each person competing against others to get ahead or to be better than them won't help to make the world better. We must all come together to solve problems, and children can learn from us the mutual problem-solving and cooperation skills that benefit everyone.

Children are capable of tremendous kindness and empathy. School-age children find ways to raise money for a social cause. Boy Scouts and Girl Scouts do things for their communities. Children can help cultivate a community garden to grow food to feed hungry families.

Adolescence: Feeling, Experiencing, Identifying and Deciding on Identification

The process of indecision is a developmental phase. In this crucial stage, in addition to "feeling, experiencing, and identifying," our adolescents are in the process of "identifying with their identifications." However, they are really in the state of "indecision." They do one thing one day, and maybe completely contradict themselves the next. It is a step that links childhood and young adulthood. But this in-between step can cause dips and leaps. An acquaintance of mine, a mother of four, once said to me, "Childhood is the icing on the cake. We parents roll up our sleeves when they are in adolescence. This is when the real work begins." I was impressed by her insight.

Indeed the real work begins, not by constantly micro-managing their comings and goings, because adolescents are becoming more independent, but by knowing when to help them and when to let go. If we hold on too tightly, our adolescents will rebel, and letting them go without supervision will leave them out in a jungle of chaos.

The balancing process that our adolescents are going through is finding their inner equilibrium when they are in a state of disequilibrium. Their maturing physical bodies, their changing hormones, their thinking abilities (or seeming lack of them) and their peer affiliations are all vying for attention. Our adolescents answer these calls with inconsistent behavior and by being dogmatic, rebellious and impulsive. The pressure on them is enormous, with too many different road signs pointing them in conflicting directions.

However, our adolescents are merely considering what to identify with, making very few final decisions. All their experiences and feelings, as well as whatever they were attached to in their childhood, are now converging on a critical point: the decision about what will be part of their identity. Our adolescents are terribly indecisive about this, which is hard on them—and us.

From my work with children and teens, I know that old unresolved and unfinished business from their childhood can turn into a crisis for adolescents. Whatever unresolved emotional issues they had earlier will escalate. For instance, if an adolescent experienced several different critical issues earlier in life—such as parents divorcing, death in the family, abandonment, neglect or abuse—those unresolved issues will hang over their feelings, and their thinking will be more confused. The child will feel and react to those old problems more deeply. The reactions may express themselves in various ways: school truancy, extreme cynicism, self-destructive behaviors or socially destructive behaviors. On the other hand, positive experiences—such as family happiness, love, affection, responsibility and so forth—will help them keep their inner equilibrium stable while they go through many changes. Those areas that gave them the most pain and the most joy are what they continue to identify with, and more strongly.

Therefore, what we parents do matters a lot at this critical point. Our attitudes and expectations are important, because adolescents strongly react to them. If we expect them to fail, they are likely to; if we have faith in them, they will try to have faith in themselves. Our expectations and attitudes hold the key to success in getting through the adolescent process. Our negative attitudes can also contribute to their difficult behaviors. Sometimes we need to be more gentle and patient with them, and sometimes we need to use tough love. Tough love is taking a hard stand, saying no and setting very firm limits. The boundary is clear and the consequence of crossing that boundary is also clear.

Somewhere along the road, our love for our maturing children and their love for us will enable us to walk each other through this critical and difficult time. We don't give up on them so that they don't give up on themselves. Our empathy and compassion is ultimately the force that binds and heals the relationship between parent and adolescent during this challenging time. As for myself, when I learned to listen to my son from my heart, I began to understand him better.

Adolescents have a great capacity to uphold ideals as well as to make trouble. If all we see and react to are adolescents' difficult behaviors and their impossible attitudes, we will fail to perceive the sweet angel still inside. Adolescents are capable of making much trouble for themselves, as well as contributing benefits for themselves and others.

The troubles they get into sometimes have dire consequences. For example, school truancy and academic failure can mess up their future career endeavors; teenage pregnancy has lifelong consequences; drug and alcohol abuse require treatment, and abstinence from addictive substances becomes a lifelong struggle; childhood neglect, abandonment or abuse can set the course for many self-destructive behaviors. Finally, the lack of love, a feeling of emptiness and anger can ripple pain through their lives. The angel is still inside, waiting opportunities for self-expression, but in the midst of too many troubles, it is silent.

For many adolescents who have not had a difficult and painful childhood and who do have a stable, loving family, their innocence still shines. Adolescents have enormous capacity to be generous, judicious, loving and kind. With greater physical independence, they are able to participate in constructive and creative projects and to help others. They are idealistic about global peace, the environment, and social justice. They can have an adventurous spirit, wanting to travel the world, if they have the opportunity. Finally, they have the capacity for compassion.

If we parents remind them of these idealistic qualities by demonstrating our own values, will our adolescents be motivated to act to make this world a better place? Instead of focusing on the negative, we can work with the positive. In other words, encouraging compassion and kindness in adolescents can help them to see beyond their own problems. Their angel inside can shine its Inner Light on the path in a confusing world.

To self-actualize, using psychologist Abraham Maslow's term, is to live to one's fullest potential. In order to do so, one must have faith in oneself, in goodness, and in the ability to fulfill one's dreams. The environment in which a child grows can be full of darkness and of conflicting messages. With the help of her parents, she learns to walk the path, sometimes on rocky roads, on roads with no signs, on roads with detours and dead ends, and on uncharted roads. We parents take our young ones' hands and gently guide them to a good start. We love them and make them feel safe.

I hope that little five-year-old boy, whose family loved sports and he did not, had a chance to find his own talents and fulfill his own dreams.

14. THE LOVE THAT BINDS

~

We may dream of walking in a beautiful garden of roses on earth, but what we often find is dirt and mud overgrown with weeds. The path is never straight and walking is difficult; the roads have missing signs. The boulders are so huge that we can't move them or walk around them. We have to climb over them to move forward. Such are the challenges in life. Only our determination and courage will get us through.

Some children come into this world with immense suffering, right from the start. Some babies are born with physical challenges and congenital conditions. Some children face serious problems living in extreme poverty and deprivation; some children and teens face multiple losses through their parents' divorces and deaths; and some have physical and mental handicaps and other challenges. Yet, their spirits can be strong and resilient. These angelic souls come into this world agreeing to face those challenges, perhaps to learn something known only to their souls. They have their inner spirit to help them to endure and overcome. We parents, too, have angels inside us to assist these brave souls on their earth journeys. Our unconditional and pure love is the powerful energy that can guide us in parenting.

For families who have adopted children, the bond between a parent and a child can run very deep. The loving bond is stronger than genes. Families coming together through adoption are not random; it is often meant to be. It is possible for those who believe in past lives to also believe that the parent and child had pre-existing bonds and that their love is rekindled through adoption. Furthermore, those families who have adopted children from other nations have wonderful opportunities to expand global consciousness, to show that we share more in common than we have differences.

Almost everyone knows someone who has lost a child. The grief and pain of losing a young person is universal. When I was a graduate social-work intern at a hospital, I worked with a couple whose four-year-old son was having an inpatient evaluation for his alleged aggressive behavior toward his peers in his nursery school. His parents, who were in their thirties, came in for an interview. When they walked into the room, I immediately felt as if an elephant had also walked in. Their faces showed tremendous pain, but their grief was silent and heavy. As the interview progressed, they began talking about the recent death of their baby daughter. A few months before, their six-month-old daughter had died from Sudden Infant Death Syndrome. They could not talk much about it; instead, they talked around her death by blaming each other for their son's aggressive behavior.

We wonder why some children leave so early. There are no rational answers, and the only answer is the acceptance of things that we cannot change. What I do know is that the love between a child and parent is powerful and eternal. A departed child's spirit is always with his family, providing unconditional love.

However, in cases of death through suicide, the deceased ones have ended their lives by their own hands, and not according to their pre-destined plan. Such an act creates a karmic debt in which the soul has to return to a similar situation to rework his problems. Clearly, suicide is not an acceptable way to handle life's difficulties, because it does not solve any problems. The pain continues for the one who committed suicide and also leaves much emotional grief and guilt for the survivors. There are other ways to deal with the immense personal pain. Personal perseverance and self-love make a difference in turning difficult corners in life. And hard times do pass away in the cycle of life changes. Compassionate outreach from others is also vital to helping the suicidal individual. But sometimes there is nothing we can do; the pain is deep inside the person and cannot be reached. We can pray for him.

For those who have lost loved ones, the truth is that the spirit of love is always alive. In our three-dimensional reality, it is hard for us to grasp this truth when we cannot see or talk with our departed loved ones anymore. Yet, if we look deeper, they are alive in our hearts. In the situation of death where the parent's soul and the child's soul are separated on different sides of life, this love truly lives on.

The music and words of John Lennon have always been part of my life. I love his music and the person he was, but I never expected spiritual communication with him. He has come to me in my dreams, or he would talk telepathically with me because I could sense his presence. Whenever I wanted to give up my writing of this book, Lennon showed up and encouraged me to persist. On the 25th anniversary of his passing, the television news remembered him all evening. While sitting in the family room watching television, I suddenly felt his presence. He said that the world was thinking of him tonight, but who was remembering Sean and Yoko? He asked me to pray for them.

John Lennon insisted that I share a message with readers of this book. He told me not to worry about believability, because he knew who those readers would be. It bought me to tears when I heard his loving words. He wants to tell others how much he, on the Other Side, loves his son, Sean. Both experienced the pain of violence and sudden separation. John Lennon tells me that it has been emotionally difficult for him as a father to be separated from his son, especially during Sean's growing years. He has struggled to accept his physical separation from Sean, but his love for him is forever.

John Lennon voiced his most personal feelings to me. Right after his message, I found a *Time* Magazine interview with Yoko Ono (September 16, 2013). Yoko acknowledged how difficult the loss of his father has been for Sean. In my heart, I know that the purpose of John Lennon's life and death was to achieve a higher purpose for humanity during this critical time of global change. His mission through his music and his messages has raised greater social consciousness in people.

Love never ends. Pure and unconditional love is the Light that binds, gels, heals and transforms. It has the energy force to bring even the most disparate challenges to a unifying direction. We may not understand why we are faced with so many struggles. What we do know is that love is all there is, with wisdom of its own to achieve the best outcomes. Together with love, we slowly overcome our difficulties. The angels inside us are always speaking.

15. TOWARD A GLOBAL CONSCIOUSNESS

~

A Shift In Awareness

Love truly begins with loving others and ourselves with fewer conditions and greater compassion. I am thinking of September 12th, the afternoon of the day after September 11, 2001. As I walked to the train station, I asked Gregory for the meaning of the World Trade Center catastrophe. He said that each one of us has to re-evaluate our priorities: who and what are most important. We could not change the event that had happened, but we can and must change from within, and that work is in our heart. We can affect each other more than we realize.

There is a Japanese legend about the 100th monkey. On an island off Japan, a group of monkeys had learned to use the stone as a tool to break open nutshells. The monkeys learned this technique from one another; soon 99 monkeys were using it. Then one day, the 100th monkey on another completely isolated island knew of this technique. What happened and why? The explanation is that the collective unconscious energy of 99 monkeys increased to such a level that it extended to another island. The 100th monkey caught on to this idea without any contact with the other monkeys.

Invisible psychic energies, which are positive and negative, are all around us. They are like inaudible sound waves rippling through the air that only some can hear. For example, dogs can hear sounds that humans cannot. Radios can intercept sound waves to channel broadcasts. We all can sense invisible energy, sometimes called *vibe*, around us. For instance, we get an impression of strangers right away through the vibrations they emit and how we receive them. Right away we can sense if they are friendly, defensive or aggressive.

Haven't we all had the experience at one time or another of a friend calling us when we think of this person? We say this must be just a coincidence, but this is unlikely. Somewhere in the psychic sphere we are both picking up each other's thoughts. Just think how advertisements on television influence the subliminal mind of their audience. If a picture is flashed multiple times over a period of time, this image is likely to get into the subconscious mind. If enough people recognize, develop and use this kind of psychic sensitivity to promote love and peace, they can bring a shift that can change many others.

For a shift to occur, Barbara Marx Hubbard, in *Birth 2012 and Beyond: Humanity's Great Shift to the Age of Conscious Evolution,* writes,

"Some intriguing science suggests that 1 percent of any solution or structure can be enough to shift the pattern of the whole."[10] However small this number is, only a tiny percentage is significant in making social change. This shift can reflect the ways people feel, think and act. For example, if one person out of one hundred, or ten out of one thousand, has made such a shift to generate love and peace, then it would eventually have impact on multitudes of other people. My Spirit Guide, Gregory, says that the biggest shift needed in this world is the change in our hearts.

Paramahansa Yogananda, (1893-1951) the great Hindu guru, brought Kriya Yoga to America in the 1930s. He wrote: "Equality cannot be established by force, it must come from the heart."[11] He meant that more violence does not build the path of peace and equality, but love does. The shift in awareness is that we are essentially One and that compassion is the healing force to transform earth's consciousness to greater peace.

The Voice of Gregory

Gregory points out that humanity is at a very critical point of change. We can either turn ourselves around or continue destroying each other and the Earth. Because we live in a world shrouded in violence and negativity, we do so much damage both to the Earth and to other human beings. Gregory's voice through me and into this book began with the horrendous event of September 11th. One swift cut of a sword has sliced open our blinded reality. Many years later, we are still picking up invisible debris that will never be completely cleaned up. Our psyche has been wounded, but our resilience is far greater.

- *On September 11th*

In 2010, on the ninth anniversary of 9/11, Gregory gave me this message:

"The September 11th event marks a momentous shift in consciousness among people, for better or for worse. Although many people still see this event in duality of us-against-others, many more are beginning to realize the necessity to bring peace and harmony. We in Heaven have observed that many of you are reaching out to one another with kindness and compassion."

"Those who lost their lives in the World Trade Center are very brave souls who sacrificed their lives for a higher purpose, that is, to promote love and peace to the world. They are the heroes to be honored and remembered. They are the

fathers, mothers, husbands, wives, sons, daughters, relatives and friends who streamed out of the physical world with the loving purpose of adding Light and Love to humanity. They are helping the world to move toward the spiritual awakening. Their love for humanity is unconditional, and is the same love that keeps them watching over their families and friends whom they have left behind. Their love is forever. For those families and friends who have agonized over their sudden departure from earth, their departed loved ones are safe in Heaven."

"Everyone has the power and the responsibility to bring peace. Awareness of the love in the little things said and done would create the millions of points of Light that the world needs to shift from global darkness to Universal Light. The choice is yours. Look within. The answers lie in your heart."

• *On Spiritual Awakening*

Gregory encourages us to have hope. He says,

"Humanity is at a turning point to a spiritual awakening. God promises you all the hope of peace and harmony, but each one of you must realize this and live it. A quickening of Light is now pulsating the Earth, moving her to a new height of higher spiritual consciousness: the oneness of humanity. How fast you all get there depends on each person. You will all reach the same destination, but not everyone is traveling the same speed or roads. Many of you are now receiving the Light. Some already enlightened souls are here to show the way."

"Spiritual awakening must begin at the heart, the first door to higher consciousness. Then another spiritual door of enlightenment will open. Love is the fundamental fuel for your travel. Awakened love is the power that will heal and transform the world. Who you are is essentially a vessel of God's love."

"There never was a time when you didn't exist, and never a time when you will cease to exist. It is only a matter of time before you are awakened to your true spiritual nature."

- *On Our Children*

Gregory shares the wisdom in our children. He says,

"Your children are the future ambassadors of peace and their hearts are the bearers of the Love that guides it.

Every child is born an ambassador of peace. In the heart of his spirit, he has the purpose to contribute to global peace through his life on earth. His dreams and talents are intricate parts of this universal peace mission, if the child does not lose his way and forget his dreams. Even children with physical or mental handicaps are on a peace mission, in which their handicaps stir others' compassion."

"In their hearts your children bear the 'inner compass' to peace, the torch that has been held by you parents. What you do and believe, how you see the world, and what you teach your children will affect how they will use their inner compass. Connect with them heart to heart so that they will hear you. Show them and guide them. Love them unconditionally so that they will model your love."

"Someday your children as adults will be in the position to contribute to greater love and peace in the world. What would it be like if these adults in whatever future roles they play are compassionate and responsible? What if these future citizens follow their hearts that guide their thoughts, feelings and actions? What if an individual sees his life as more than what is in it for himself and includes

others in his thoughts and actions? There certainly will be less selfishness, less thoughtlessness, less deception, fewer mistakes, greater trust and better outcomes. With enough people who think and act this way, the world will move forward in peace to a spiritual awakening."

Concluding Words

The shift to more compassion and greater peace doesn't happen overnight. Progress goes up and down, not in a straight line, but hopefully toward an upward trend. Many of us act more like Sisyphus, the legendary king of Corinth. In Hades, Sisyphus was condemned to roll a boulder uphill, only to have it roll down again as it neared the top. Up and down the hill he went, but going nowhere. We parents labor hard to raise our children and do our best for them. In the foggy mist of the Earth's darkness, our best efforts oftentimes go in conflicting directions. We try but remain baffled, as if we cannot go above our starting point. However, through unconditional love, we can move to higher ground.

Through love, we will become one. Love breaks down barriers, divisiveness and hatred. People's hearts can be strung together through the thread of empathy and compassion. The heart is the center in which humanity is to heal and be transformed. We need to take out the fears, the hostility and hatred and to replace them with understanding and compassion. Love is peace that begins with oneself and in the family and then ripples outward to the community and the world.

Epilogue

Into My Father's Heart

While my father's dementia was increasing, his thoughts went in conflicting directions, reflecting his endless worries and fears—real or unreal. One day, I held his hands and said, "Dad, your memory is not good. When you are quiet and calm, think of me in your heart. There I will always stay the same and be here for you." Although his eyesight and hearing were diminishing, he heard me.

Just like when my young son asked me if I still loved him when I was angry at him for not picking up his toys, my father echoed the same uncertain sentiment. One of an elder's greatest fears is abandonment.

My father really grasped my words. Thereafter, he often remarked to me with a smile, "I remember you in my heart!" He seemed to understand things in his heart that his mind could not: pure love is steadfast, trusting and reliable. We were both connected heart to heart, where we heard each other. My love got into my father's heart, and his into my inner child's heart. Before he passed away at the tender age of ninety-eight, his last words to me were, "Agnes, I love you. I depend on you!"

Acknowlegements

As a writer writes, the Universe conspires to bring people to support her work. Thus, she never writes alone without inspiration, coaching and critique from caring individuals. First, I thank Kathleen Spivack, award winning poet and accomplished writer, who, upon reading my first draft, astutely pointed out that I had bigger stories between sentences: I found my voice. Her unwavering support and encouragement over the years has led me to believe that I can make a contribution. Also, my dear friend and colleague, Jan Wiley-Egdall, patiently critiqued my manuscript again and again, year after year. Her friendship is one of my greatest blessings.

I thank my editor, Lawrence Kessenich for his skillful editing and friendship of the spirit. I appreciate Susan Schmidt Ph.D for her expertise and fine critique that reflected her sensitive, novelistic style of writing. From them, I have learned so much about writing and editing.

My thanks goes to artist Eujin Kim Neilan who did the beautiful cover illustration that eloquently captures the essence of my book, and to Karen Lawson-Chipman, who exquisitely designed the front-back cover.

I thank my husband, Ken, and my son, Graham for their

overwhelming love and support. Ken has been my tireless frontline editor, never complaining how many times he has to read the same old paragraphs and chapters. I thank Graham for allowing me to share our stories, and his patience in reading my manuscript.

I express my love and gratitude to my dear mother and father who shaped my many life's stories. Through all the good and hard times, our love shines and lives on.

I am grateful to many individuals who share my dream that we can create a more peaceful and kinder world. I thank the Spirit of John Lennon for pushing me not to give up writing this book, when many times I almost did. Last but not least, I send my gratitude to my awesome Spirit Guide Gregory for his faith in me before I had it in myself, and for his powerful voice throughout the book.

Endnotes

1   Lisa See, *Snow Flower and the Secret Fan* (Random House, 2005).

2   Barbara Mark and Truly Griswold, *The Angelspeake Book of Prayer and Healing,* (Simon and Schuster, 1997).

3   Antoine De St. Exupery, *The Little Prince,* (Harcourt, Inc. 2000).

4   *The Holy Bible*, Revised Standard Version.

5   Michele Pierce Burns and Danson Mandela Wambua, *Danson,* (St. Lynn's Press, 2009).

6   Dan Millman, *The Laws of Spirit,* (New World Library, 1995)

7   Mattie J. T. Stepanek, *Heartsongs*, (Hyperion, 2002).

8   Tobin Hart, *The Secret Spiritual World of Children*, (Inner Ocean Publishing, 2003).

9   Thomas Armstrong, *The Radiant Child*, (The Theosophical Publishing House, 1988).

10 Barbara Hubbard, *Birth 2012 and Beyond*, (Shift Books, 2012).

11 Paramahansa Yogananda, *A World In Transition*, (Self-Realization Fellowship, 1999).

About The Author

Am I a human on a spiritual journey, or am I a spirit on a human journey? Why am I here? Since childhood these questions have persisted in my mind. A masters in social work from Boston College allowed me to look at what is the meaning of family. I became a social work supervisor at a child welfare agency that matched Big Sister volunteers to Little Sisters; there I saw the variety of needs in families, some of which our volunteers could provide. Within this agency, I also directed a special volunteer program that reached out to children and teens in the Boston Chinese Community, where many struggling families were immigrants. In another agency setting that provided counseling to troubled families with children, I observed so much suffering and how people were caught in a cycle of violence that often went from generation to generation. Later, when I became a parent, I loved raising my child but there were challenges, too. I searched for an understanding of my experiences and observations. Divine Spirits heard me; their telepathic communication with me provided much insight, and the Universe began opening up to me. The shocking event of September 11th was the turning point that inspired me to look deeper for peace in a world that knew little of it. From that time on, I saw myself as a spirit on a human journey.

Printed in the United States
By Bookmasters